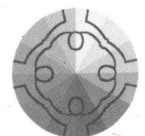

Ancient Rome!

Exploring
the Culture, People
& Ideas of This Powerful Empire

Avery Hart & Sandra Gallagher

Illustrations by Michael Kline

Williamson Publishing • Charlotte, VT

Library of Congress Cataloging-in-Publication Data

Hart, Avery.
    Ancient Rome! : exploring the culture, people, & ideas of this powerful empire / Avery Hart & Sandra Gallagher ; illustrations by Michael Kline.
      p. cm.
    "A kaleidoscope kids book."
    Includes index.
    Summary: Examines the history, geography, culture, and politics of the Roman Empire and similarities to the United States.
      ISBN 1-885593-60-0 (pbk.)
      1. Rome—Civilization—Juvenile literature. 2. Activity programs in education—Juvenile literature. [1. Rome—Civilization.] I. Marks Gallagher, Sandra, 1945- II. Kline, Michael P., ill. III. Title.

DG77 .H34 2002
j937—dc21

2002026819

Kaleidoscope Kids® Series Editor: **Susan Williamson**
Illustrations: **Michael Kline**
Interior Design: **Sarah Rakitin**
Cover Design: **Black Fish Design**
Cover Illustrations: **Michael Kline**
Time Line Research: **Jean Silveira**
Printing: **Quebecor World**

Printed in Canada

Williamson Publishing Co.
P. O. Box 185
Charlotte, Vermont 05445
1-800-234-8791

10 9 8 7 6 5 4 3 2

Dedication
This book is dedicated to teachers, librarians, and others who instill the love of reading and literature in children.

Acknowledgments

Thanks to Paul and Matt Mantel for their patience during my extended imaginary trip to Rome, to Clayton for devising ingenious projects, to Sandy for a lifetime of friendship, to Dr. Gerald Fegan of Penn State for his expertise, and to Susan and Jack Williamson, who have done so much to support creative thinking and spread the love of learning to children everywhere!
— A.H.

I'd like to thank Joey Gallagher, Jr. for his excellent project ideas and Latin translations. My thanks and all my love to my husband Joe, my family, and my dear friend Irene for their unwavering support and belief in me.
—S.G.

Photography/Illustration: page 13: "Aeneas Fleeing Troy," Scala/Art Resource, NY; **page 17:** "Capitoline She-Wolf," Timothy McCarthy/Art Resource, NY; **page 26:** arch illustration, Danny Yee; **page 36:** Temple of Vesta at the Forum Boarium, Scala/Art Resource, NY; **page 48:** Roman Forum, Romer/Explorer/ Photo Researchers; **page 50:** Roman Forum, Bertinetti/Photo Researchers; **page 52:** Pantheon, Laurie Platt Winfrey, Inc.; **page 54:** Appian Way, Mulvehill/Photo Researchers; **page 56:** Roman aqueduct, Art Resource, NY; **page 70:** "Julius Caesar Proceeding to the Senate on the Ides of March," Giraudon/Art Resource, NY; **page 73:** Apartment building, SEF/Art Resource, NY; **page 74:** Roman mosaic, Sarah Rakitin; **page 75:** Roman baths, Susan Williamson; **page 81:** Roman Colosseum; Susan Williamson; **page 84:** Maritime Theatre at Hadrian's villa, Laurie Platt Winfrey, Inc.; **page 87:** Piazza San Pietro, Vatican City, Sarah Rakitin

For more Williamson Publishing books by Avery Hart, please see page 96.

Contents

The Great Parade of the Past

Imagine a long "Parade of History," with participants from the earliest cave people to technicians and office workers of today. The floats showcase the great accomplishments and inventions of all humankind.

Listen and look! Here come the ancient Egyptians, beginning with farmers who march to the sound of wooden flutes. On their first float, a leader, called *pharaoh*, sits calmly as slaves fan him with leaves. Then comes a float with a model of a pyramid and another showing the invention of paper. Best, though, is the final Egyptian float, where children release birds into the air to celebrate Egypt's long stretch of peace.

Next come the ancient Greeks on a float designed as a sailing ship. Then, a group of Greeks walks by, proudly holding a banner that reads DEMOCRACY! What a great gift from the Greeks! Aristotle, Socrates, and Plato — three wise thinkers — are next. They wave to the crowd that cheers their amazing mental powers.

The Greeks have several floats celebrating the arts: The theater float has actors wearing masks of happiness and sadness; others feature poetry, music, and dance. When a float with lifelike marble statues passes by, everyone sighs in delight.

Alexander the Great, wearing a turban and orange robe, holds up a globe as if he owns the world.

Aha, here come the Romans! At first, we see a few farmers, but eventually a large number of noisy people in colorful dress pass by. Some wear togas; others wear clothing from faraway lands. Some march in line as soldiers, some as priests, and yet others march in chains, held as prisoners and slaves. The Roman procession is one of many moods: solemn and serious in part, merry in other parts, and sometimes even rowdy.

One Roman float displays a court of law; another shows leaders — senators, generals, and kings. Their engineering floats are showcases for roads, bridges, and aqueducts. The engineers are proud, standing tall and waving to all. A display of architecture shows temples and palaces with *domes* (vaulted ceilings).

What a magnificent parade of history that travels right to modern times! We begin to realize that some themes — such as greed, power, human rights, revenge, religious freedom, and inventiveness — have been around for a long while; some for better, others for worse. And though there are gems of wisdom that have been passed along the time line of history, so, too, have pieces of ignorance, and with them, intolerance.

No people contributed more of both wisdom *and* ignorance than the Romans. Wouldn't it be awesome to march with the Romans, if only in your imagination? What might you treasure from the experience? What would you want to discard?

Come along, then, and fall into step. We'll march together to the beat of life in Roman times.

JUST FOR FUN!

Speaking of the "gifts that keep on giving," here's one of the more obvious gifts — Roman numerals!

Go on a quick search in your home, school, or in a mall to count how many places you find Roman numerals.

To refresh your memory, in Roman numerals,

I = 1	L = 50	D = 500
V = 5	C = 100	M = 1,000
X = 10		

To read Roman numbers, follow these rules:

▣ When a numeral of equal or lesser value immediately follows a numeral, add them.

(Example: **VI** = 5 + 1 = 6;
XX = 10 + 10 = 20)

▣ When a numeral is immediately followed by one of greater value, subtract the first from the second.

(Example: **IV** = 1 from 5 = 4;
XL = 10 from 50 = 40)

In Search of Ancient Rome:
The Place & Time

So, you've joined the parade of history, stepping into Roman times. There are floats and people for miles and miles in front of you and farther than the eye can see behind you.

As you approach the parade line, you hear some Romans arguing. One of them, a dignified gentleman in a white toga, shakes his finger angrily at the group standing around him, "We Romans united the world! We left magnificent gifts for those who came after!"

But a woman in a tattered robe responds bitterly, "You bullied the world and thought you were better than everyone else. You left misery for your slaves and the poor."

To your amazement, the crowd nods in agreement — with both of them! They all seem to understand how two different parts of human nature could have existed in the same people, at the same time. Understanding the Romans means seeing how they were smart, and *not* so smart. How they were generous, and also selfish and greedy. How they could be hard workers, and also be spoiled and lazy.

But there are no two ways about the lasting impact that Romans had on world history: It was — and is — huge!

Roman History: a Snapshot

The Roman world began with the city of Rome around 750 B.C. (approximately 2,750 years ago). Once the city was established, the Romans began taking over the neighboring tribes. After 400 years, they controlled most of Italy.

During a 50-year burst of conquest, they expanded to an empire on the three continents of Asia, Europe, and Africa. By about A.D. 200, the Romans ruled three out of every four people in the world!

The huge empire then split into halves: East and West. The West faded first, but all told, Roman power lasted over 2,200 years.

Search a Globe for the World of the Romans

At its height, the empire's landmass was as large as the United States today! To find the Roman world on a globe or map, look for Italy, on the continent of Europe. It sticks out into the Adriatic and Mediterranean seas, as if Italy is "kicking" the island of Sicily! The city of Rome is near the center of Italy.

Look all around the Mediterranean Sea. (*Mediterranean* means "middle of the earth.") In Roman times, every place around this sea came under Roman rule.

Look up and left for the island of Great Britain, where England is located. Look down and right for Syria and Israel, called the Middle East. *Those places, too, and everything in-between, made up the Roman Empire.*

Try It! How many modern-day countries can you count where the Roman Empire once existed? Make a list of the ones we mentioned, and check a map or globe to identify the others. There are *lots* more!

Do you live in a place where the Romans once ruled? Do any of your friends or relatives come from one of these places?

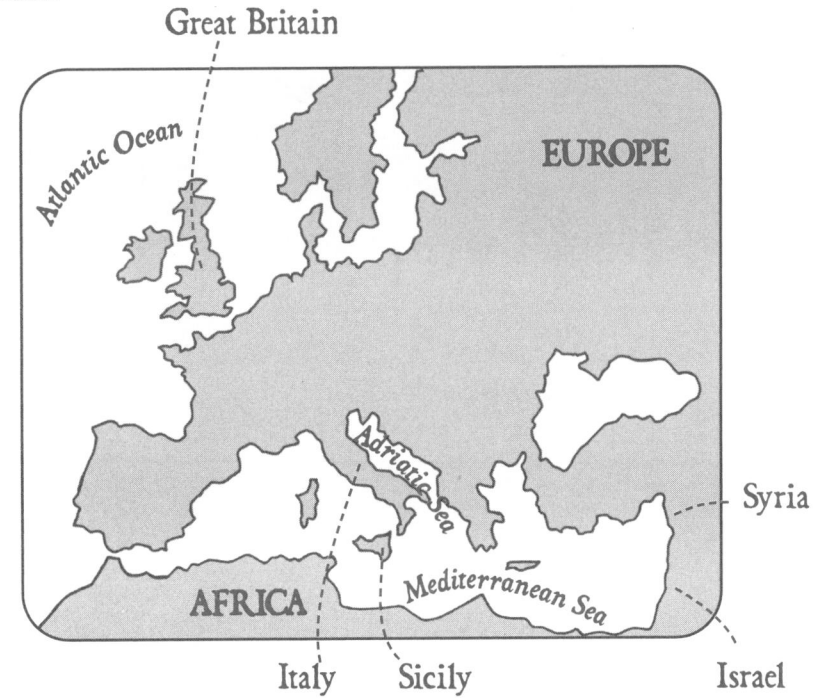

Make an Across-the-Centuries Map

Mapmaking can be a lot of fun, especially when you are about to make a map that spans the centuries. Use the maps shown here by tracing them and then enlarging them (see below).

Please remember: Don't write in this book. It spoils it for others who use it after you. Thanks.

▦ First, on a piece of 8½" x 11" (21 x 27.5 cm) paper, we'll make a map that shows the land (and surrounding waterways) of Asia, Africa, Europe, and Great Britain.

▦ Next, we'll draw the outline of the Roman Empire, when it was largest, *circa* (which means about) A.D. 200, onto those landmasses.

▦ Then, we'll make an overlay, on a piece of transparent paper, of a modern map, showing the countries that are there today.

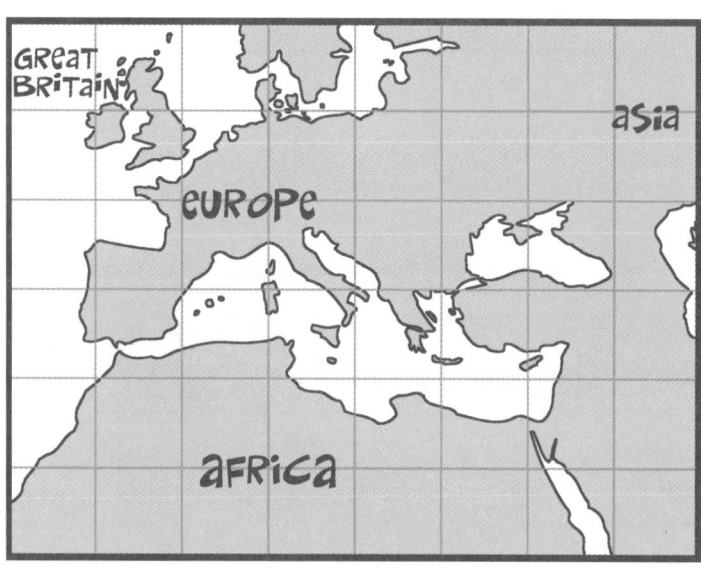

LANDMASSES OF ASIA, AFRICA, EUROPE, AND GREAT BRITAIN

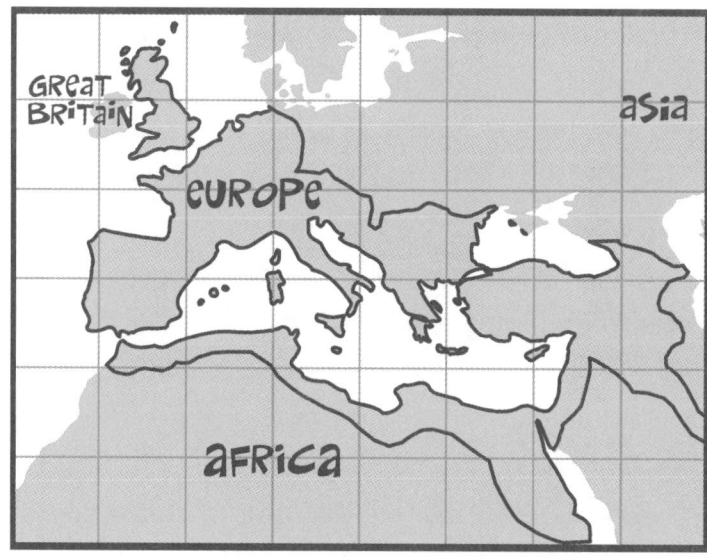

OUTLINE OF ROMAN EMPIRE, CIRCA A.D. 200

Make It LARGER!

Here's an easy way to enlarge maps. With a ruler, mark an even grid of squares onto the map you wish to make bigger. Now, draw a grid of larger squares onto a larger piece of paper. Working with one square at a time, transfer the lines in each of the smaller squares to the larger ones. You'll end up with the same map, only bigger!

Map Talk

Maps can practically talk! They tell us about the past so that we can understand the present. In Portugal today, for instance, you'll see sidewalks and buildings covered with colorful mosaics made with little pieces of stone or tile arranged in artful designs. Some mosaics are very, very old and some are new. Your maps tell you that the Roman Empire included Portugal, so you can probably figure out why mosaics are still popular in Portugal today! See how maps "speak" to us?

Global Unity

Did you notice in the parade that the Romans wore not only togas but fashions of faraway lands, too? The Romans created the first *global society*, made up of people on different continents.

Today, we live in a global society that includes the whole planet. Keeping world peace is one of the greatest challenges of our global age. Also, we trade products with people of other continents; we share ideas about cures for illnesses, and we work together to keep our planet clean and green.

Have you "gone global"? Do you think of yourself as a citizen of the world, as well as a citizen of the country you live in?

Try It! How global is *your* world? Find out by looking for items in your home or school that were made in other countries. Check the labels on the clothes you are wearing. They may have come a long way to get onto your back!

Look at the bottoms of objects to find their country of origin. How many things did you find that were from different countries? Surprised? You may be sharing your space with a whole bunch of global objects — not to mention ideas!

Time Changes

B.C. AND A.D.

We better get this straight or we'll be lost in time forever! There's a big difference between 2000 B.C. and A.D. 2000 — 4,000-years difference! You see, time moves along a continuum (picture it as a line).

The counting of time in the Western world grew from the early days of Christianity, with the number "1" standing for the year that Christians believe Jesus Christ was born. With that birth as a dividing line, anytime before is called B.C. — before Christ. Anytime after is A.D., *anno Domini,* Latin for "in the year of the Lord." The year 100 B.C., for instance, stands for 100 years before Christ's birth. The year 100, or A.D. 100, is 100 years after Christ's birth.

What Year Is It?

We better march a little faster, because time is passing us by in this parade! Just as the Roman Empire spanned three continents, it also spanned a very long time — over 2,200 years! So how old are YOU? And have you changed a lot in those years? Now, just imagine what happened in ancient Rome. The people at the beginning of the parade must be very different from the people at the end of the parade, because time changes a lot of things.

Try It! Just for fun, visit with an older person — someone the age of your grandparents or of an elderly neighbor. Ask this person about life when he was growing up. Did his family have a car? What about a TV? How much did a loaf of bread cost? Could he phone a friend in another country? Did he have an e-mail pen pal? Be sure to share what you do in your everyday life, because older people love to get to know kids of today!

You can see for yourself how much can change in the span of one person's life, let alone the thousands of years of the life of a country or an empire.

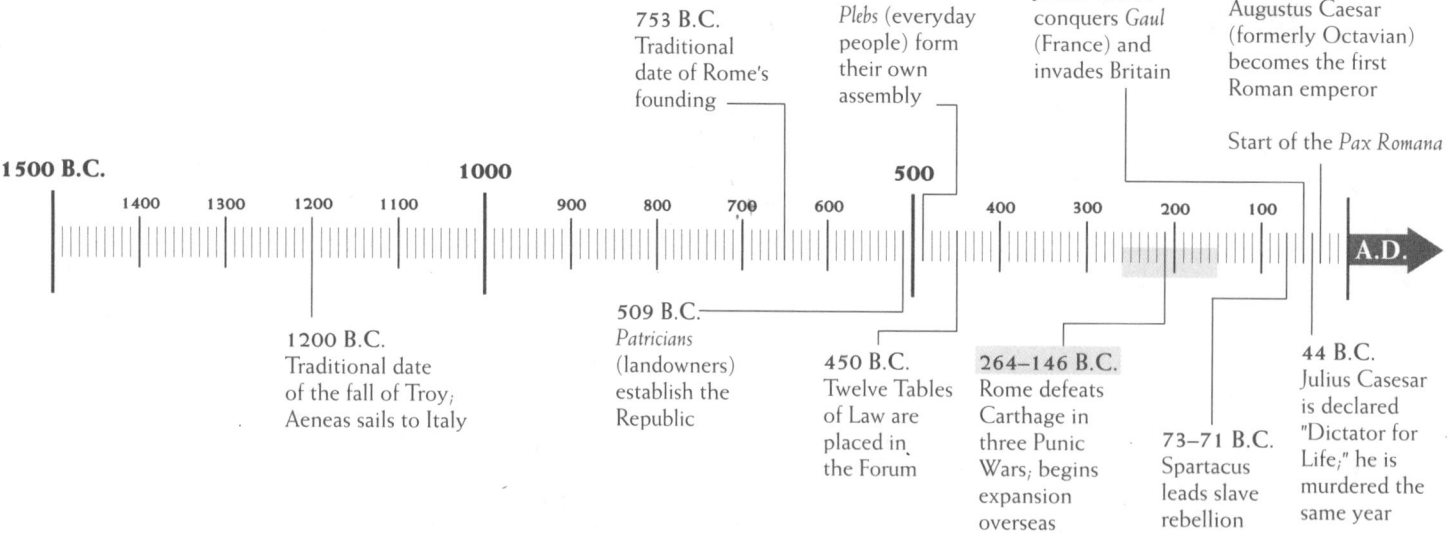

753 B.C. Traditional date of Rome's founding

494 B.C. *Plebs* (everyday people) form their own assembly

58–51 B.C. Julius Casear conquers *Gaul* (France) and invades Britain

29 B.C. Augustus Caesar (formerly Octavian) becomes the first Roman emperor

Start of the *Pax Romana*

1500 B.C. — 1400 — 1300 — 1200 — 1100 — 1000 — 900 — 800 — 700 — 600 — 500 — 400 — 300 — 200 — 100 — A.D.

1200 B.C. Traditional date of the fall of Troy; Aeneas sails to Italy

509 B.C. *Patricians* (landowners) establish the Republic

450 B.C. Twelve Tables of Law are placed in the Forum

264–146 B.C. Rome defeats Carthage in three Punic Wars; begins expansion overseas

73–71 B.C. Spartacus leads slave rebellion

44 B.C. Julius Casesar is declared "Dictator for Life;" he is murdered the same year

Why Can't We All Get Along?

In the great parade of history, we saw that there were both good and bad passed along. Learning from history means avoiding the troubles of the past, and refusing to accept ideas that lead to no good. The Roman parade has treasure to enjoy, but also trouble to avoid, such as love of power, greed, and lack of creativity.

Some of the bad stuff continues in the form of *ignorance* (lack of understanding and knowledge), *intolerance* (thinking that certain groups of people are better than others are), and *injustice* (treating people unfairly). Because of this nasty trio, people of the world continue to live in fear of each other, in fear of violence, and with hunger and preventable diseases.

Try It! Let's each begin in a small way, to make our part of the world — our classroom or our street or our household — more peaceful and accepting. Say hello, share outgrown toys and clothes, lend a helping hand, donate canned food or vegetables you grow in your garden to food shelters.

Want to help kids like you in other lands? You can join an organization like Childreach or the World Ark that will connect you to kids in other lands. Through the World Ark, you can even help a hungry family get a chicken, rabbit, goat, or cow. (Find them at **<www.heifer.org>** and **<www.childreach.org>**.)

We each *can* make a difference!

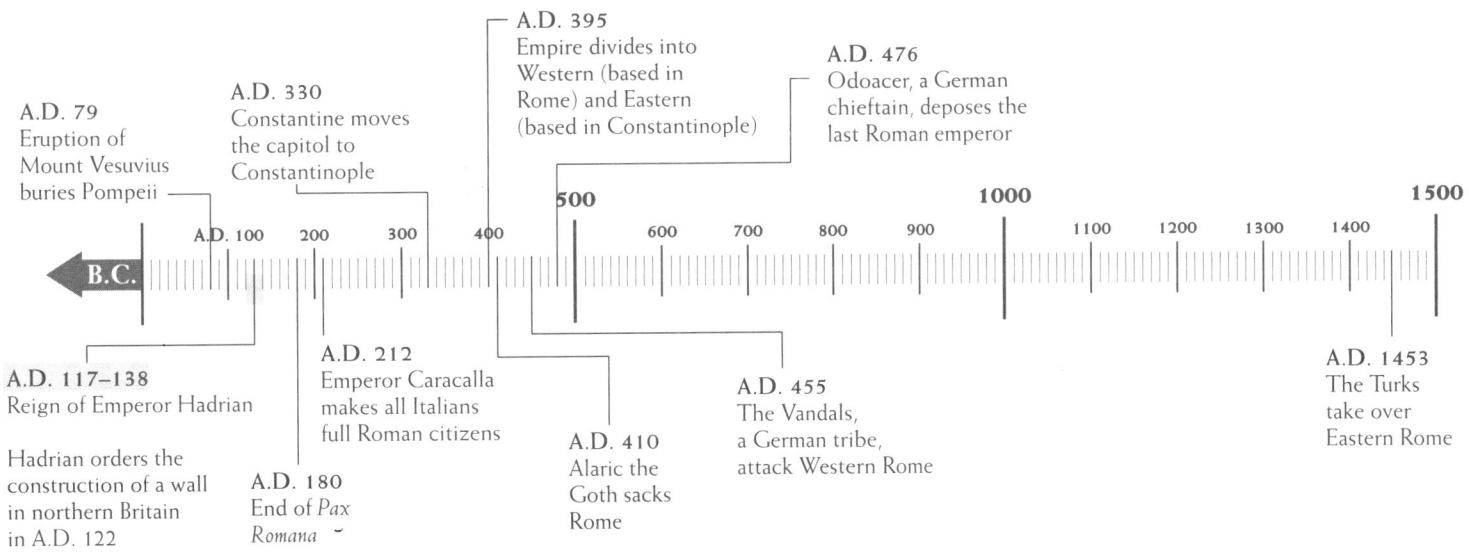

Discovering Rome's Ancient History:
Investigate, Participate & Relate

"Aeneas became a wanderer, but the Fates were preparing a big destiny for him."

—LIVY, ROMAN HISTORIAN

You're at the beginning of the Roman section of the parade, when suddenly a flame shoots up over the parade route. Clouds of misty fog follow the fire-burst; through them, you see the shadowy figures of a man and his son, walking alone.

What's the meaning of it all? People around you say that the fire symbolizes the burning of the city of Troy, supposedly destroyed by the ancient Greeks. Roman legend says the last Trojan to flee was a soldier, named Aeneas (eh-NEE-as) who sailed to Italy with his young son to begin what would become the Roman civilization. The clouds hang heavy, making it difficult to see, just as is true of the early days of Roman history that are almost totally lost in the fog of time!

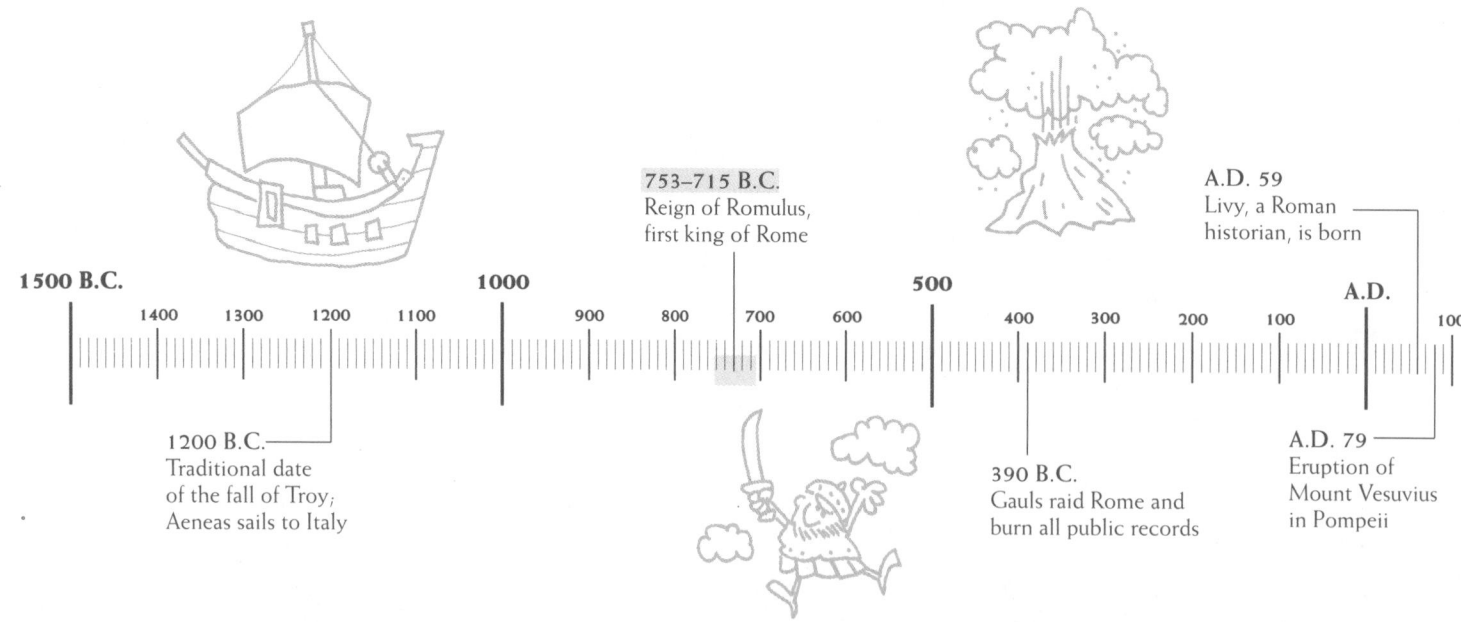

753–715 B.C.
Reign of Romulus, first king of Rome

A.D. 59
Livy, a Roman historian, is born

1500 B.C. 1400 1300 1200 1100 **1000** 900 800 700 600 **500** 400 300 200 100 **A.D.** 100

1200 B.C.
Traditional date of the fall of Troy; Aeneas sails to Italy

390 B.C.
Gauls raid Rome and burn all public records

A.D. 79
Eruption of Mount Vesuvius in Pompeii

"Aeneas Fleeing Troy" with his young
son; Pompeo Batoni (A.D. 1708–1787)

Accurate history can be lost for many reasons. So how did Romans lose theirs? Good question!

In 390 B.C., the *Gauls,* who lived in the land we now call France, smeared mud on their naked bodies and raided Rome. They stole what they wanted and burned all the rest, including all public records! So much for recorded facts of Roman history. That means we have to use other resources that historians have turned to over and over in their pursuit of the truth.

Tools and Techniques of Discovery: Curiosity, Evidence & Sources

Discovering ancient history is detective work, and to be a smart detective, you need to use tools and techniques to piece together the information you collect. To begin, you need *curiosity,* for without it, there is no motivation to discover how people lived, what they were like, and how their lives all those years ago impacted our lives today.

And you'll search *for evidence* that comes in two forms: *Primary evidence* is anything created *during the time* being examined. The very best primary evidence in Roman history is Pompeii, the buried city (page 18).

Secondary evidence is information that came later, such as a letter or poem written about Rome at another time after the Roman Empire, or a photo of an ancient vase.

Detectives need *sources,* too, in the form of legends and folktales written about a certain time in history. But a smart detective knows that some sources are more reliable than others. The same is true in history: Knowing your sources lets you judge how reliable the information is.

Ask the Questions

As you explore the Roman world, you'll find yourself sorting through heaps of *stuff* — facts, legends, evidence, lists of people, recipes, poems, battle plans, *theories* (ideas), descriptions of buildings, customs, places, and events.

A good question to keep in mind is,

What does it all mean?

A second question to keep in mind is,

Why do I even care?

Put those two questions together and you get to the heart of the matter:

What does it all mean to me?

With that question front and center, let's continue along this parade route to see for yourself if Roman history has anything to do with you and your life today.

And Now the Fun: Investigate, Participate & Relate!

Imagine a stone castle with a thick iron gate that can never be opened. When you peer through the rusty keyhole, you see part of the floor, a bit of the ceiling, and maybe a corner of a picture hanging on the wall. But you *know* the castle has whole floors and rooms that are completely out of view.

History can be a lot like that huge castle, for there are big chunks of history missing — or at least out of sight. The fun comes in finding pieces and putting them together to arrive at some understanding of what the people of that time and place were all about. You see, history is really *not* about *stuff*: History is about people. And that's where, per-haps, you will find how it relates to you today.

Try It! To get an idea of what we can — and cannot — know about the past, bring a notepad outside. Your mission is to write down *observations* about life *inside* your house or school, *using only what you can see from outside.*

You may see a sofa and chairs, for example. Look closely; does it look like people have been sitting on them? Can you tell the ages and interests and even the weights of the people who were in the chairs? Any eyeglasses nearby? A book? Knitting needles? Toys? Observe and note all you can.

Now comes the tricky part: Pretend that what you see is all you know. Use your observations to create a scenario about life inside the house or school. How close is it to your real experience as a person who lives there?

Livy

"It is heaven's will that my Rome will be capitol of the world!"

—Romulus, supposedly "quoted" by Livy

Meet Livy, (formally Titus Livius) who wrote Roman history to remember, as he put it, "the deeds of the foremost people of the world." He completed *The History of Rome* in 142 volumes, 35 of which still exist. These are real treasures of history, but there's some trouble with using them as evidence.

- First, Livy wasn't alive in the early days of Rome. He was born in 59 B.C., hundreds of years later.

- Second, he wanted the people of his day to be proud of their past, so he never wrote anything unflattering about the early Romans.

- Third, he accepted legends (such as the one you are about to read) and beliefs as truth. What does that do to the value of Livy as a source for secondary evidence?

Investigating Legends

Why bother with stories that people may have made up thousands of years ago? Well, for one thing, stories are fun. For another, legends (no matter that they are unproven) tell us about the values, customs, behaviors, beliefs, and other traditions of the people who tell them. We can find out what the people feared and what the people wished for.

When you read the following legend about the founding of Rome, you will find, not only an amazing story, but also many clues to Roman values. See what you can discover about what the Romans thought about power, pride, people, and what was most important to them.

The Legend of Romulus and Remus

Once two royal infants, descendants of the Trojan hero Aeneas, were left to die at the edge of the Tiber River because a jealous uncle wanted to inherit their throne. Just as the babies were about to drown, a she-wolf rescued them and nursed them, as her own.

One day when they were toddlers, a shepherd saw the twins playing under a fig tree in the woods. He adopted them and named them Romulus and Remus.

When they were teenagers, the boys got in some trouble and had to go before a judge. The judge immediately realized from their clear speech and good posture that these could not possibly be the children of the shepherd. He concluded that these boys were the royal twins who had been abandoned as babies, long believed to have died.

When the twins learned about their past, they set out bravely to settle the score. They restored their grandfather, the rightful king, to his throne. Then they began their search for a new kingdom of their own.

Inviting any males who wanted to go — shepherds, servants, and slaves — they searched for the fig tree where they had once played. It was found growing on land within seven hills. Romulus wanted to build the great city on one hill, but Remus had his eye on another hill. The brothers prayed for a sign about who should get his way in selecting the kingdom-to-be's site.

Remus spied six birds flying over head. Then Romulus said that he saw twelve! Remus thought *he* should have *his* way, because he saw the birds *first*. Romulus thought *he* should have *his* way, because he saw *twice* as many.

Remus was angry, but Romulus ignored him. Romulus went ahead and put on special robes and began acting as if he were a priest. He told the men to dig a holy circle that was called *mundus*, meaning "world." All who wanted to join him must throw fruit into the circle as proof that they would all share the "fruits of the land." Then, Romulus plowed an outline of his city and began to build a wall around it. He told everyone to stay away until the wall was finished.

But Remus leaped over that wall, saying, "Look! So easy!" Obviously, the wall wouldn't keep enemies out.

With that, Romulus attacked his twin brother — and killed him! He announced that his city would be named Rome — named for himself. Anyone who insulted him or his city would be put to death!

And so it is told.

THE SHE-WOLF WITH ROMULUS AND REMUS; AN ETRUSCAN BRONZE, CIRCA 5TH CENTURY B.C. THE SHE-WOLF IS ANONYMOUS; THE TWINS WERE ADDED LATER, BY ANTONIO POLLAIUOLO.

Think About It!

When Siblings Fight

Romulus and Remus argued about who was first and who saw most. Sound familiar? But there must have been another way to resolve this conflict!

When Remus got angry, he didn't say why. Instead, he taunted his brother. When Romulus got angry, he became destructive (to say the least!).

These brothers needed help in communication skills. How would you help them resolve this situation? Do a role-play of Romulus and Remus. How would you defuse the situation? Now, role-play that you are a mediator, helping them resolve this issue.

Go Undercover — If You Dare!

Well, sibling relationships don't seem to rank high in the Roman values portrayed here! But what values do you think *were* important, as shown in this legend? What customs can you pick out of this bizarre story? If you were assigned to go undercover in Rome at this particular time in its history, what would this legend tell you about Roman values, so that you could "fit in" like a good undercover investigator? Remember you have to behave like the people did back then, get accurate information, and escape with your life!

Pompeii: Extraordinary Primary Evidence

Talk about time-travel! The city of Pompeii in Italy is an historical investigator's dream of primary evidence! You see, Pompeii had been a popular seaside resort city until life — and time — literally stood still in A.D. 79. That was when the famous volcano at Mount Vesuvius erupted, burying Pompeii and its people under layers upon layers of volcanic ash.

Digging Pompeii out, more than 1,500 years later, archaeologists discovered the city just as it had been on that August afternoon when the volcano blew! Loaves of bread were in the bakery. Tables were set for lunch. Carts were in the streets. Political posters were on the walls. For this time and place, we had much more than a keyhole to peek into; we were invited into the homes and onto the streets, stepping back into that precise moment in time. How extraordinary and eerie, too!

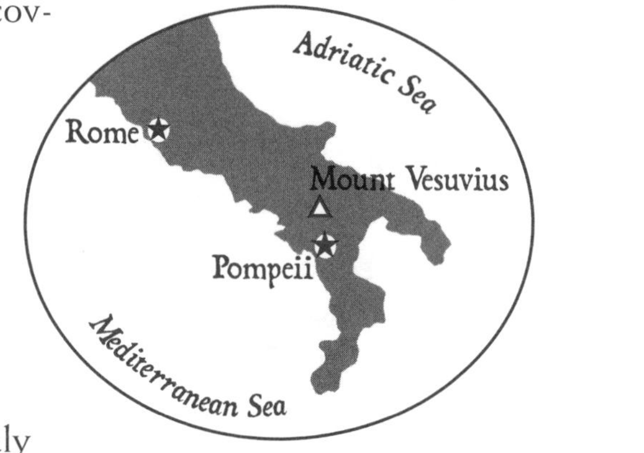

How was Pompeii found? Quite by accident, as is true of many archaeological discoveries. One day in A.D. 1592, a farmer who lived in Italy near Mount Vesuvius began digging a flat rock out of his field. After lots of effort, he realized that the "rock" was actually a rooftop! He had just discovered the buried city of Pompeii!

Two Ways to Tour Pompeii

▦ Take a virtual tour on-line at
<www.thecolefamily.com/italy/pompeii/slide01.htm>.

▦ See Mount Vesuvius from the U.S. space shuttle at
<volcano.und.nodak.edu/vwdoc/volc_images/img_vesuvius.html>.

Map labels: Adriatic Sea, Rome ✪, Mount Vesuvius △, Pompeii ✪, Mediterranean Sea

Go on a Dig!

An *archaeologist* studies the ancient past by piecing together fragments of bone, pottery, and other remnants. Archaeologists look for clues to the past in rocks, soil, and even garbage dumps!

Many of the greatest archaeological discoveries have been made by ordinary people just like that farmer who kept digging to satisfy his curiosity. You may not discover an ancient city buried in your backyard, but hey — you never know!

Get a trowel, or a shovel, and a sifter (like the kind you play with at the beach), and see what you can find (with permission). We found a seashell in our backyard — and we live more than 20 miles from the ocean! How'd that get there? What will you find, and what will it "tell" you?

You'll need patience on your dig — and so do real archaeologists. Actually, you are doing exactly what they do: dig carefully, sift, dig, and sift.

The Two Plinys

Pleased to Meet You

Pliny the Younger and his uncle, Pliny the Elder, were highly educated patricians with villas in Pompeii. For a heart-stopping account of the eruption — in which the Elder perished — check out Pliny the Younger's letters, written to his friend and famous Roman historian, Tacitus. (Search the web for Pliny the Younger: 'Eyewitness to the Eruption of A.D. 79!'.)

As the parade passes it's plain to see that many different kinds of people made up the Roman population. Banners announce the names of the different tribes of Italians — and even Greeks — that became part of the Roman world. Way in the distance, you can make out a float with men wearing golden crowns. Could it be Roman royalty? Let's go see!

A Quilt of Many Cultures

"All that you see here, Stranger,
where mighty Rome now stands,
was grass and hills ..."

—PROPERTIUS, ROMAN POET

High on a group of hills in the country of Italy stands the city of Rome, or *Roma*, to those who live there. Today, Rome is a busy city, with streets full of cars, taxis, bikes, and buses. Millions live there, and more come to see beautiful carved fountains and fabulous old cathedrals, to hear great music, and to walk through the ruins of ancient Rome that still stand in the heart of the city.

But once — thousands of years ago — the seven hills of Rome were empty grassland. The only life then were grasses, plants, trees, wolves, birds, bears, and a few human beings who lived in mud huts, doing their best to survive.

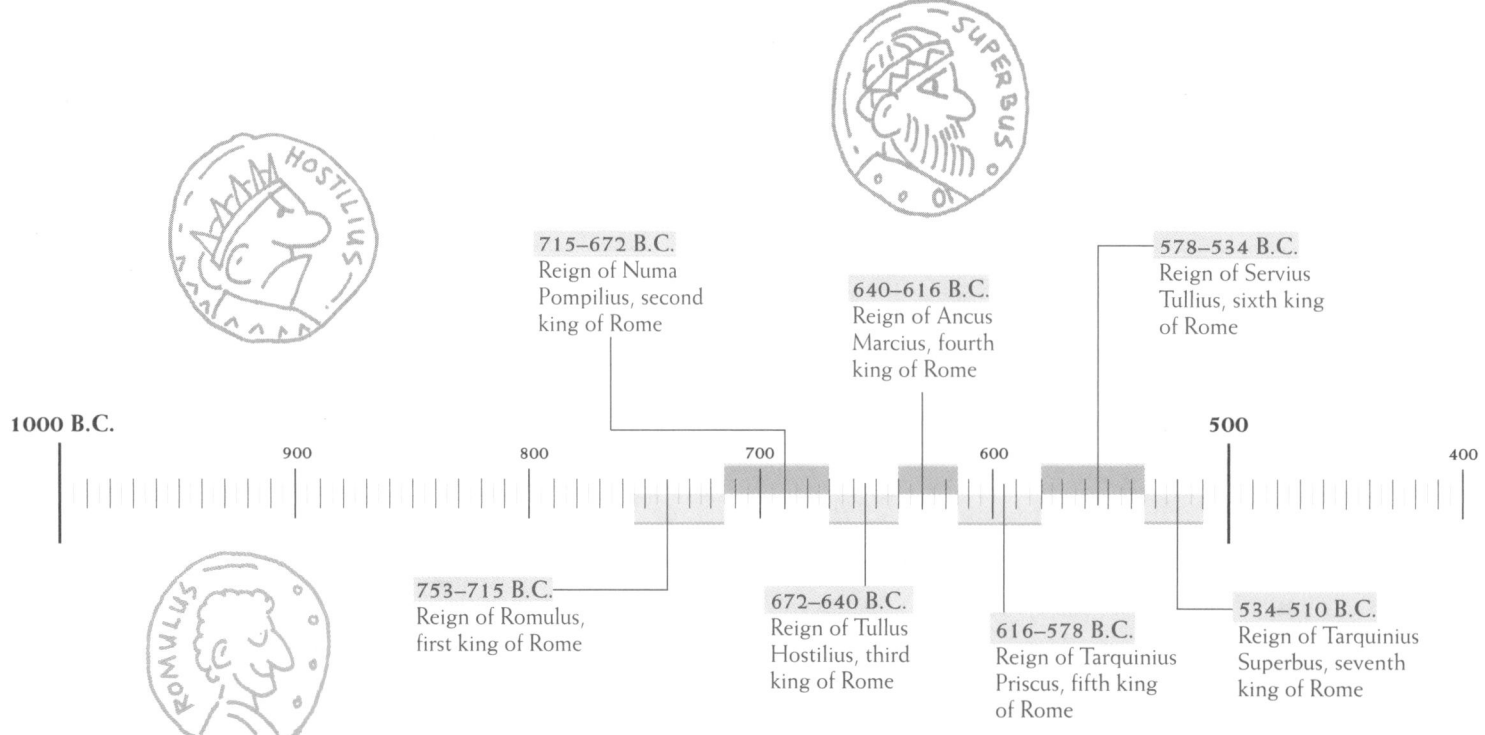

715–672 B.C.
Reign of Numa Pompilius, second king of Rome

640–616 B.C.
Reign of Ancus Marcius, fourth king of Rome

578–534 B.C.
Reign of Servius Tullius, sixth king of Rome

1000 B.C.
900
800
700
600
500
400

753–715 B.C.
Reign of Romulus, first king of Rome

672–640 B.C.
Reign of Tullus Hostilius, third king of Rome

616–578 B.C.
Reign of Tarquinius Priscus, fifth king of Rome

534–510 B.C.
Reign of Tarquinius Superbus, seventh king of Rome

Italy was a good place to live in ancient times. It had plenty of fresh water and sunshine that made it ideal for growing food. It had oceans, plentiful with fish and seasides with a mild climate, appropriate for year-round living.

No wonder the sunny peninsula attracted dozens of tribes, each with its own way of life. Even the ancient Greeks, who seemed to know a good thing when they saw it, established a city there, in the south. One way or another, in time, these groups would all yield to Roman power. Some resisted and fell after bloodshed; others joined the Romans, voluntarily, or semi-voluntarily.

After 400 years, even those whose ancestors resisted were on Rome's side. The Italians became the Romans best friends and strongest allies. From those humble beginnings came the great Rome, and far more. Our world has never been the same since.

The Tribes of Ancient Rome

"Romulus made a safe place for the surrounding people, a miscellaneous rabble eager for new conditions."
—LIVY, ROMAN HISTORIAN

The "rabble" that Livy mentions were actually the first people of Italy. One by one, their tribes would first fall in battle to Rome and then, in what may be one of Rome's greatest legacies, they would become part of it.

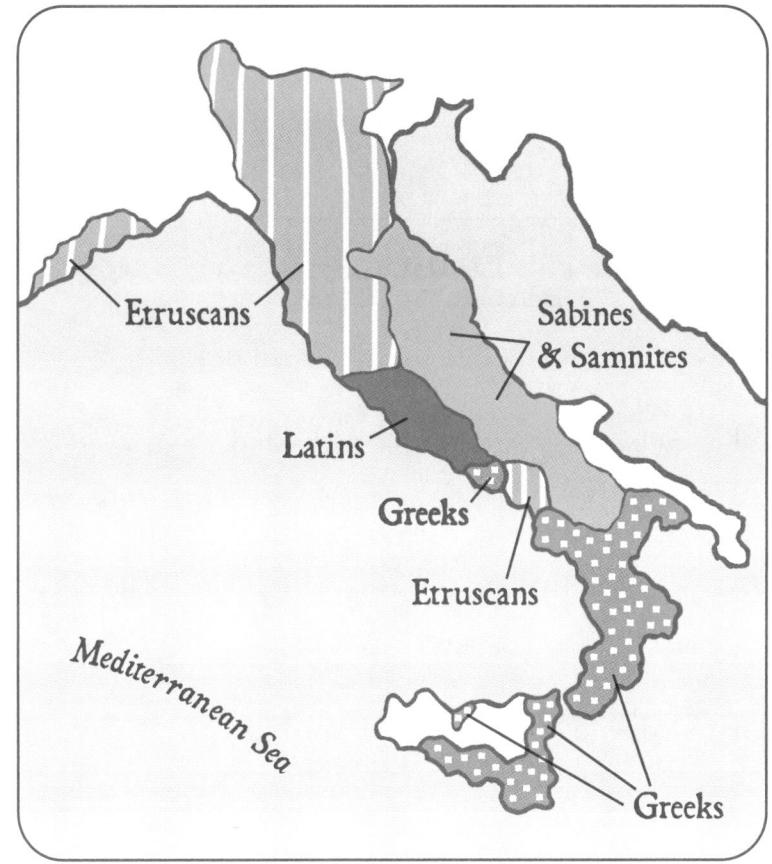

MAP SHOWING THE LOCATIONS OF
THE TRIBES OF ANCIENT ROME

Sabines and their cousins, Samnites

- mountain people from south of Rome

- excelled at growing grain

- fierce warriors who once defeated the Romans

- Sabine women (supposedly) were the first Roman wives (page 24)

- gave Romans a love of discipline and strength

Latins

- lived in Latium on the hills and plains

- had good farmland, but were open to attack

- unified as "the Latin League," a very modern concept for protection

- gave Romans the gifts of government and language (pages 27–28)

Etruscans

- lived in Etruria, on the coast, north of Rome

- ruled by kings with purple robes and gold crowns

- introduced the horse-drawn carriage and hand cranks to the Romans

- traded with the Greeks and worshiped Greek gods

- created beautiful art

- gave Romans their religion (pages 29–30)

Ancient Greeks

- established colonies in southern Italy and Sicily

- were more skillful, artistic, and richer than the Italian tribes

- were much admired by the Romans and Etruscans

- gave Romans literature, art, style, math, and philosophy

Play Roman Tag

To show how the Romans united the tribes of Italy, play Roman Tag. Start with a group of kids, each taking the name of a tribe. "IT" is Roman. When IT tags a kid, they join hands and together try to tag another "tribe," who then also holds on. Continue until you have a group of kids, all joined by hands, chasing the last remaining "tribe." When everyone has been tagged, everyone is Roman, but each person is also who he was before he became Roman!

Need names for more players? The Romans also conquered Italian Volscians and Umbrians.

P.S. Did you notice anything about joining together? A group — whether of kids playing tag or of countries joining together — works much better if the members work together, moving toward the same goals. But when everyone tries to be the leader or sets her own goals, it is impossible to get anything done! Hmmm.

Gift of the Sabines: The First Roman Wives

The Sabines were one of the tribes of early Rome. According to Livy, the Sabine women were the first to marry and have children with Roman men. He writes that Romulus lured the Sabine tribe into Rome for a festival and games. Then, "upon a signal, the Roman youth ran different ways to carry off the girls by force. A great number were carried haphazard, according as they fell into their hands."

We've turned the legend into a rap, because many raps today are about harsh stories made to sound like they are acceptable behaviors, even when the behavior and actions are unacceptable, as was this kidnapping.

The Kidnap Rap

Now Romulus was lonely and so were his men
'Cuz every Roman rooster had to have a Roman hen.

But the Latins said, "No!" when asked for some brides;
The Etruscans and the Sabines also failed to provide.

So Romy asked the Sabines to a picnic and some games
'Til he broke up the party by grabbin' the young dames!

Romy shouts, "Yo, Sabines, you really oughta split! —
We need some females, and your daughters are it!"

The Sabine men got some weapons to go back to fight
'Cuz kidnapping their daughters, man, that ain't really right!

Then the Sabines made a battle, on the very next night.
They planned on really fightin', with all their brutal might.

But the battle broke up quickly when the Sabine chicks appeared
Saying, "Daddy, please don't hurt 'em, 'cuz it ain't like you feared.

The Romans really rocked us when they stole us away
But they're treatin' us real good now, and WE WANNA STAY!"

P.S. The Sabine king and the Roman king, Romulus, ruled together for six years, until the Sabine king died.

The Triumphal Arch

To begin their rule together, the Sabine king and Romulus walked under a ceremonial arch together. And, when visitors came to ancient Rome or soldiers returned from battle, they walked under certain ceremonial arches, too. The first of these arches were simple semicircles of bricks and stones. Later, the Romans made them thicker and put decorations on them, celebrating victories in war.

Although the Romans weren't the inventors of the arch, they used them in all sorts of building. Freestanding arches had a spiritual meaning for the superstitious Romans. They believed that walking under one would "cleanse" a person's spirit, making him peaceful and honest, and thereby ready to join the great Roman city.

Make a Roman-Style Triumphal Arch

The basic Roman arch is built starting at the *abutments,* or end supports. Stones are added to both sides, higher and higher along the curve, until only one more stone, called the *keystone,* is needed at the top.

The Romans realized long ago that it's impossible to make an arch without supporting it as it goes up. They used a wooden frame, called the *centering,* to support arches as they were being built. The centering was removed after the keystone was placed.

To build a Roman-style arch, you'll need some clay, Play-Doh, or ready-mix concrete, and a bunch of same-sized rocks.

Use something as the centering for your stone and clay bridge. Perhaps you have a block that's the right shape. Or try cutting up a cylindrical container (a rounded oatmeal container works well) to get a curved surface. Then, using the clay as cement, fit the rocks together over the centering to form your arch.

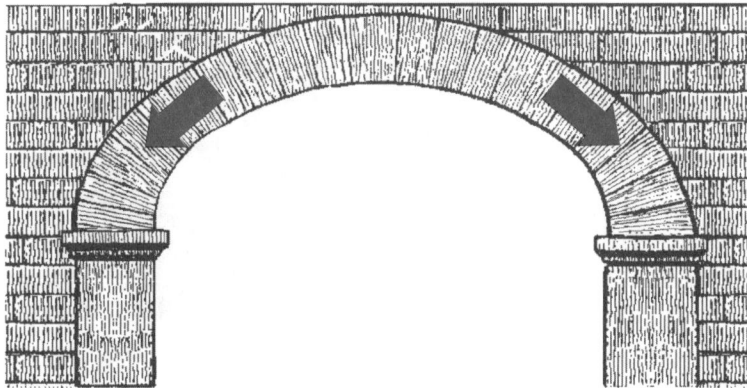

How It Works!

An arch's beauty comes from its graceful curve. Its strength comes from how this curve carries *load* (weight) outward in both directions to the abutments at its ends.

Since everything is pushing and being pushed at the same time, all the parts of an arch are *compressed* (squeezed).

Stone is super strong when it's compressed, but it's weak when it's pulled, or under tension. So ancient builders figured they could span longer distances using stone arches instead of stone beams (which are both pushed and pulled). What a great observation those early builders made!

Building Strength from Weakness

The famous Italian artist Leonardo da Vinci once said, "An arch consists of two weaknesses which, leaning on each other, become a strength." What a wonderful image! The two weaknesses are the arch's two halves, but when leaned against each other at the top stone, or keystone, they become strong by the force of compression. Only then can the arch support itself.

What do you think Leonardo da Vinci's observation means when applied to life in general?

Gifts of the Latins: A Lasting Language

Though not many people speak Latin these days, it was the language of ancient Rome, and like so many things, it has become a part of the Roman legacy that is alive and well today. Latin is used in law, in much of science (including medicine and botany), and even on our money. In fact, it is found in a lot of the words English speakers use every day.

But what Latin and its *root words* (the words that are used to form other words) can tell us about ancient Rome is a fascinating tool for historical investigators like you. Let's take the Latin word *pater*, which means "father," for example. Now, as you'll realize when you meet the people on page 34, in Roman families, the father had a huge amount of power. In fact, he had the power of life and death over his children!

So when the Romans devised a three-part government, who got the most power? The *patricians*, that's who! Without knowing anything else about Roman government, you could use that language clue to understand the power of the patricians, because of its root word *pater*.

Worldly Words

DISCOVERING ROOTS

These English words — and more — come from *pater*, the Latin word for "father." Can you figure out what they mean now that you know their Latin root word?

PATERNAL, PATERNALISM, PATERNITY, PATRIOT, PATRIOTISM, PATRONIZE, COMPATRIOT

"Mom" was *mater*, which is also the root of English words. How many can you think of? Now, hunt for a dictionary to see how well you did!

ti amo!*

TUNA FROM ITALY

*ITALIAN FOR "I LOVE YOU!"

Worldly Words

A LITTLE ROMANCE

After Roman times, the Latin language that the Romans spoke mixed with tribal languages to make modern-day French, Spanish, Portuguese, Italian, and Rumanian. (Look back at your Across-the Centuries map, page 8, to understand more about these languages. See, maps *do* talk — in French, Spanish, and Italian!) These languages, spoken by hundreds of millions of people today, are called *Roman*ce languages because of their *Roman* roots.

When Did You Learn Latin?

Even after the era of ancient Rome, Latin remained the language of educated people all over the world. With a common language, people from different lands could share knowledge without confusion. When Carl Linnaeus, a Swedish botanist, decided to name and classify all the plants in the world, he gave them Latin names to end confusion over their local names.

But here's the best part: Even if you've never studied Latin, you practically speak it already! That's because about 40 percent of English words have Latin roots.

Try It! Here are some so-called English words that are actually Latin:

do, color, condo, quiet, honor, multi, sane, insane, ridiculous,

rare, unique, accuse, apparatus, pauper, furor, farina

Here are some Latin words that you are sure to recognize:

introduco, immenso, magnificus, absentis, hilaris, accelero, gloria, humanus, excellentia, frivolus, delectabilis, rudis, miserabilus, offero, publicus, voluntarus, respondo, occuro, necessarius

For fun, write a silly or serious story, poem, or rap using as many Latin/English words as you can. Or, make up a crossword puzzle using as many words as you can, beginning with *delectabilis* in the middle.

Gifts of the Etruscans: Royalty and Religion

The first kings came from the Roman, Latin, and Etruscan tribes that began to merge in the early days of Rome. When Romulus declared himself king, he made the Etruscan religion the official Roman religion (page 16). Kings were chosen by the *patricians*, or the "fathers," as the descendants and close friends of Romulus were regarded. Each king was head priest, top judge, and army leader. During the time of the kings, the city of Rome was built.

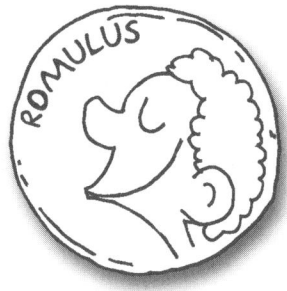

Language Link

🔲 *Romulus* and *Rome* (but you knew that). If he named a city after himself, he must have thought he was pretty hot stuff!

🔲 Does the name *Pompilius* remind you of the Latin words *pomp* (fancy ceremony or parade) or *pompous* (very showy and self-important)? So, what's the clue?

🔲 No need to point out the obvious link here. Looks like *Hostilius* lived up to his name!

The Seven Roman Kings

I. Romulus: You're not surprised, are you? After all, you didn't expect him to give up his power. He started the city and was later worshiped as a god.

II. Numa Pompilius: He built a school for priests and began the Roman religion that worshiped spirits, called *numina* (pages 37–38).

III. Tullus Hostilius: He bashed Rome's neighbors and took their lands; he was the first king to expand Rome's borders.

IV. Ancus Marcius: He made peace with the people that Tullus Hostilius fought. He also built new Roman cities in Italy. (Sounds like a good guy!)

V. Tarquinius Priscus: This Etruscan king built the Temple to Jupiter, the god of all Romans and Etruscans. (See how the Etruscans brought their religion to Rome?)

VI. Servius Tullius: A son of a slave, he rose to be a very effective and popular king, and he organized the military.

VII. Tarquinius Superbus: He and his son were so badly behaved that the Romans decided to do away with kings altogether!

   Try It! Pick one king and based only on what his name sounds like to you or tells you from its roots, draw, describe, or role-play what he would be like if he lived next door to you today.

Language Link

▨ Do you think being the son of a slave, or in *servitude*, has anything to do with Servius's name?

▨ Hmmm! *Superbus*? Well, before you say that he doesn't seem very super, look at the Latin meanings: His name means "Tarquin the Proud." He certainly was proud; so much so that the people couldn't stand his proud behavior of acting as if he were better than everyone else and could have anything he wanted. So, they ran him out of town!

Worldly Words
LANGUAGE LINKS AS CLUES?

   Are these language links really clues about the kings' behaviors? Well, consider this: Tullus behaved very badly, so the name *Hostilius* could have resulted from the people's experiences with him. And Servius *was* a slave.

   Think about the nicknames you give your friends: Do they usually reflect a quality (a good one, of course!) about them? If you called someone Be-bop, what would you know about him? What are Fast Track, The Rhyme Machine, and Giggles like?

Pleased to Meet You

Lucretia

Meet Lucretia, famed for her purity and beauty, who came to a sad end. Her problem started when her husband bragged about her to his army comrades. He spoke so glowingly of Lucretia that Superbus's son, the prince of Rome, decided to pay her a visit — a sneak visit — that turned into an awful attack. Lucretia took her own life rather than live with the memory of it! When the patricians found out what had happened, they drove Superbus and his son out of Rome. Never again, they declared, would kings, who could allow and cause such evil, rule Rome! Because of Lucretia, it is said, the rule of Roman kings came to an end!

Time Changes

MONTH BY MONTH

When Romulus was king, he divided the year into 10 months. Then, when Numa Pompilius became the second king of Rome (715–672 B.C.), he added the months of January and February, instituting the 12-month calendar.

An End and a New Beginning

After Lucretia, the Roman patricians decided to govern themselves in a new form of government called a republic. Soon, the float for the Roman Republic will pass by, but first, listen! It's the sound of laughter! Here comes a bunch of Roman kids! Join the parade now, and you may well see some familiar things.

A Kid Is Still a Kid

"Few children talk of any thing but gladiators and horses.
When we enter the classroom that's all the conversation is about!"

—TACITUS, ROMAN HISTORIAN

Here they come, Roman kids, looking as fun loving as we hope you are today! Their shouts of *"Ave! Ave!"* mean "hello," and they wave to the people watching the parade. Reading their nametags, you see Claudio and Julia, leading a pet pony. Next is Flavio, who pulls a cart, and Titus, holding the hand of little Candida, who clutches a doll made of wood. When Flavio turns and motions, Adriana runs up to him and the others, her pet squirrel hopping along on a leash. She is followed by Gaius, a young teen who proudly carries the most exotic pet of all — the one that the Romans discovered in Egypt — called a cat!

You'd probably like ancient Rome if you were a pet-loving kid. Aside from all you see in the parade, Roman kids kept parrots (who spoke Latin, of course!), nightingales, turtles, and even mice wearing tiny harnesses that pulled miniature chariots!

If you were a Roman kid, you'd play outside in the family courtyard or on a city sidewalk. You'd have balls, and toy animals and dolls made of ivory, wax, metal, or wood. You'd probably have a small cart drawn by a goat or dog. And none of your toys would ever need batteries!

Just like today, your parents would want you to be happy. You might have a swing or a wooden horse to ride. You'd play tag and marbles, spin tops, and have make-believe battles with little wooden soldiers. Older kids and adults played a kind of backgammon and were fascinated by the adult gladiator games (page 81).

Better hurry to enjoy it all, though, because Roman childhood didn't last long! By age 14 kids were supposedly all grown up! (And by age 28, the average Roman's life was over!)

Play Trigonon

Like action? Try Trigonon! (Note that *tri* means "three" in Latin.)

You'll need: at least three players and three to six balls

The play: The three players stand about 10 feet (3 m) apart, at the points of a triangle. Each stays in this place during the entire game. The balls are tossed into play by one of the players, one by one, always moving in the same direction. As balls are added, the game speeds up, like a three-person juggling act!

The win: If you have three (or whatever number you decide) misses, you are out. Then the two remaining players throw to each other, until only one person is left as the winner. Lots of kids want to play? Have a tournament with several games going at once and then have a play-off, in which the winners play each other. The last remaining player is the winner.

The Power of Papa: His Word Was Law

Life could be brutal for kids in Rome, if their fathers were mean. A newborn had no legal rights until her father picked her up and said she could live! If the father didn't want the baby — for any reason — she was left to die in the wilderness, *no matter what the mother wanted!* Some infants died, some were rescued and adopted, and some became slaves.

Roman fathers — called *pater familias* (page 27) — kept their power over their children all of a child's life, too. They could *legally* kill or sell their children into slavery — even after the kids grew up!

Fortunately, most Roman fathers loved their kids. But with the threat of the law in the background, obedience to Papa was *very big* in the Roman world.

Bulla, Bulla

Every loving Roman father gave his infant a *bulla,* a locket with a lucky charm inside, to wear around his neck. In wealthy families the bullas were gold; others were made of leather. The bulla was kept all during childhood, supposedly to protect the child from harm. Boys took theirs off when they turned 14 and were officially adults. Girls took theirs off the night before they were married.

Think About It!

Domination vs. Respect

Domination is when someone has complete power over someone else. Interestingly, the word *dominate* comes from the Latin word *domus* meaning "home," because Roman fathers had total power in their homes.

Today, in most households, the adults have some control over children because kids are not ready to live on their own yet. Children may not like all of the rules, but they obey them, understanding that the rules are there to guide them.

People obey out of trust and respect or out of fear and domination, whether at home, at work, or at school. Which have you obeyed from? If you are afraid of some adults, now is the time to discuss it with them or with someone you trust. Don't wait; do it *now!*

Worldly Words

VIRTUES

Virtue (from the Latin *virtus*) means goodness. The early Romans held many virtues to be of the highest importance and hoped their children would display these characteristics throughout life.

- ▣ **DIGNITAS:** being a worthy, or dignified, person; someone people respected
- ▣ **DISCIPLINA:** being disciplined in training; learning how to do something well
- ▣ **FIDES:** being faithful to family, government, and the gods
- ▣ **GRAVITAS:** being serious, not silly
- ▣ **INDUSTRIA:** working with a purpose, until a job is done
- ▣ **LIBERTAS:** treasuring freedom
- ▣ **SEVERITAS:** being able to go without comfort

Do you agree that these are of "highest importance," or are there other characteristics that are more important to you? Which of these traits do you think you possess? Which do you hope your friends possess?

Libertas

History, Herstory: Where Are the Women?

If you were a girl in Roman times, you would belong to your father. Unless you were extremely rich, you wouldn't know how to read or write, and no one would even think about teaching you.

When it came time to marry, your father would choose your husband, who would become your new owner after your dad died. And when historians wrote about the people of your country, you and your female friends would hardly be in the book!

But don't be fooled by lack of evidence — girls and women were half of Roman society. They helped their mothers survive when their dads were at war. They whispered advice to their husbands and brothers. They taught their children Roman ways.

"Herstory" is a modern attempt to recover the lost history of women and girls. Check out the website at **<www.historyeuropeanwomen.com>** to find a few missing pieces.

Above the Rest:
The Vestal Virgins

Only one small group of females, priestesses called *vestal virgins*, were treated as well — or better — than men. No man had power over them, and they were thought to be "above the law." Unlike ordinary women, vestals could save and spend money without permission, too.

The vestals paid a high price for their privileges, however. During the 30 long years (from ages 10 to 40) that they tended the goddess Vesta's sacred fire, they were forbidden to have any boyfriends whatsoever! And talk about harsh — if a vestal broke that one rule, she would be buried alive!

TEMPLE OF VESTA AT THE FORUM BOARIUM, ROME, BUILT LATE 2ND CENTURY B.C.

Freedom of Religion

One of the things that all children could do was observe their own religion, even if they were from a country that had a religion that differed from the Romans. We hope you live in a country where — thanks to the Romans, among others — you are free to practice any religion you choose, or even none at all. When the Romans conquered a new land, they took young men as soldiers, but they left people's religions alone.

Roman religion was a mixture of government, prayer, fear, spirits, fun, festivals, and home life. Because of this, children were involved in their religion early on.

Three Gifts from King Numa

Remember *Numa Pompilius* (page 29), the second of the seven Roman kings? He brought the different tribes together by creating clubs, called *collegia*, for people with similar interests and skills. (Your school may have similar clubs, so students with the same interests can become friends. Count that as a Roman idea in action!). Another gift from King Numa was the first 12-month calendar, based on the cycles of the moon, (later improved upon by Julius Caesar.)

But the gift he gave that the Romans took into their hearts and homes was a way of worship. He taught the early Romans to worship spirits, or life forces, that came to be called *numina* (singular: *numen*).

All through Roman history, every important event began with a message to a Roman numen.

Numina Everywhere

Numina were invisible forces of nature. Every natural action had its own spirit — even the process of rusting! The natural force of the Tiber River had a numen named *Tiberis*, and the early Romans worried that he wouldn't want a bridge built over him!

Since natural forces were everywhere, so was Roman worship — at home, in the fields, and wherever the government met. Performing ceremonies and rituals *properly* was very important to the Romans, because only then would the numina be pleased.

Hello, *Lares!* Hi, *Penates!*

Home was holy to the Romans because the family lived there, and they treasured their family life. And with each family "lived" the family numina. There were the *lares*, the spirits of the ancestors, for instance. In the pantry where food was kept, were the *penates*, the spirits of the snacks, so to speak. The fireplace, or hearth, had a sacred fire for *Vesta*, the goddess of the hearth.

Home Altars

Many religions use the home as the center of religious practices. Some have religious celebrations at special meals; others pray at certain times in the home, and still others have altars in their homes to remind them of their faith. Today, the Soka Gakkai International (SGI) is a worldwide Buddhist organization of about 18 million people, all with home altars. Their altars display a copy of an ancient drawing, a glass of clear water, a vase with green leaves, fruit, and a bell — something pleasant for every sense: smelling, seeing, hearing, touching, and tasting.

You had to keep your numina happy! Father tossed a piece of bread into the fire for Vesta at the main meal. He left some fruit for the lares, and cheese for the penates. When Rome was under attack, all over the city, the lares were given whole meals! (Of course, no one ever saw a numen, but their faith told the Romans they were there.)

Most homes had altars, or *larariums*, shaped like little temples, for the lares. Sometimes, the altar had a little statue of a boy, with fruit in one hand and a plate in the other. When father arrived home, he greeted the lares before saying hello to anyone else in the family! And the family shared all its joys and sorrows with the lares.

O, Holy Government!

Imagine if your president or prime minister was also your priest, minister, mullah, or rabbi? What authority that person would have! That's the way it was in Rome, where religion and government were one and the same. If you did something the government disapproved of, people might say that the gods were against you, too!

The Roman government's religion respected the numina, but focused more on animal sacrifice. The Romans also used *augury*, which is sensing the ways of the gods in bird behavior. Roman priests kept holy chickens. The way a chicken pecked at its food would tell them what mood a certain god was in! (Does this sound like quackery?)

⊞ Some Traditional Roman Numina and Gods

Flora: Spirit of Plants

Fons: Spirit of Spring of Flowing Water

Fortuna: Lady Luck

Janus: God of Beginnings and Endings

Lares: Spirits of Ancestors

Penates: Spirits of the *Storeroom*

    (pantry with food)

⊞ Roman Gods Borrowed From the Greeks

Apollo (Greek *Apollo*): God of Sun, Light, Truth, Music, Beauty, and Archery

Juno (Greek *Hera*): Wife of Jupiter

Jupiter (Greek *Zeus*): God of Thunder

Mars (Greek *Aries*): God of War

Minerva (Greek *Athena*): Goddess of Wisdom and War

Venus (Greek *Aphrodite*): Goddess of Love

Vesta (Greek *Hestia*): Goddess of the Hearth

Many Names for God

The Romans worshiped Jupiter and other gods; the Greeks worshiped Zeus; Christians worship Jesus; Jews call their God, Adonai; Muslims pray to Allah; and Native Americans honor The Great Spirit. There are many other names for God, too. Do you think the people in all these religions may be worshiping the same great force and only the names are different?

End of the Chapter? Then Good-bye, Janus

Janus, the first Roman god, supposedly guarded the gates of heaven. He was a double-headed god of beginnings and endings, gates and doorways, war and peace. King Numa named the month of January after him. To a Roman, honoring Janus brought good luck.

Put Janus over Your Door

You may not believe in the strengths of the Roman Janus, but hey, why not make one for fun, since he represents doorways (and you probably go in and out of them very often!)?

▓ **You'll need:** tape measure, scrap paper, newspaper, foam-core board, scissors or craft knife (use only with adult supervision), tape, art materials, picture hangers, a ladder or step stool (to hang it)

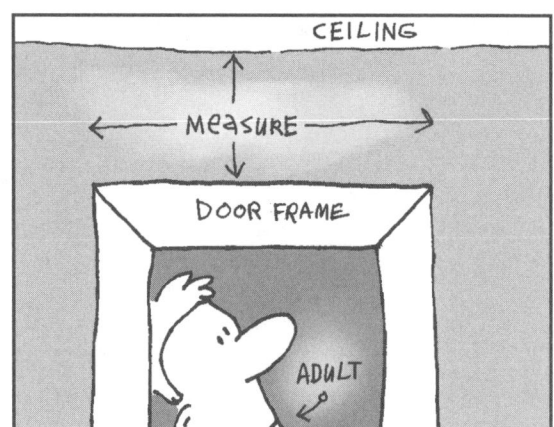

1. Measure the width and the height of the area between the ceiling and the top of the door frame so that your Janus will fit.

2. Sketch your Janus on scrap paper. Then, draw an outline on newspaper to use as a pattern. Cut the pattern, tape it to the foam-core board, and cut out the design. Fill in your Janus with paints or a Roman-style cut-paper mosaic (use little squares of paper to fill in, leaving space around each square to look like grout). Attach a glue-on picture hanger to the back, and hang it!

P.S. A Janus on *both* sides of the door brings *double* luck, so get busy!

MAKE YOUR JANUS FACING FORWARD AND BACKWARD, WITH HIS TRADITIONAL BEARD AND CROWN OF LAUREL LEAVES

Join the Parade!

Now that you've glimpsed the life of kids in ancient Rome, let's step back into the parade and onto a float to glimpse the story of the Roman Republic.

A New Republic

"Of all connections, none is more serious, none is more dear than that between every individual and his government."

—CICERO, ROMAN SENATOR

What fun to see the children and families of ancient Rome. And now, the kings have passed, and the Romans rule themselves in the first republic! Here come floats with the men who will lead the new government of Rome!

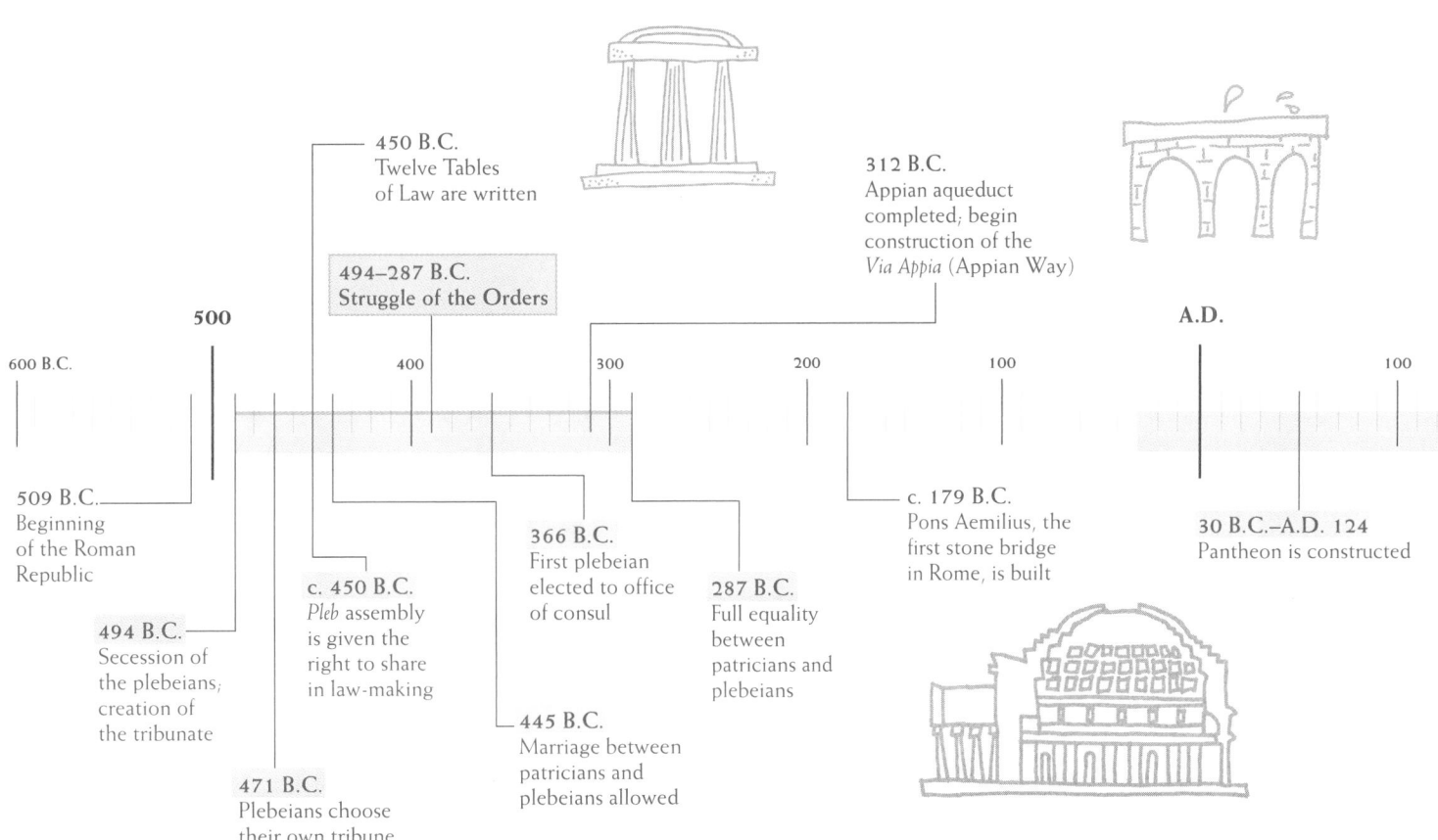

450 B.C.
Twelve Tables
of Law are written

312 B.C.
Appian aqueduct
completed; begin
construction of the
Via Appia (Appian Way)

494–287 B.C.
Struggle of the Orders

500

A.D.

600 B.C.

400

300

200

100

100

509 B.C.
Beginning
of the Roman
Republic

c. **179 B.C.**
Pons Aemilius, the
first stone bridge
in Rome, is built

30 B.C.–A.D. 124
Pantheon is constructed

494 B.C.
Secession of
the plebeians;
creation of
the tribunate

c. **450 B.C.**
Pleb assembly
is given the
right to share
in law-making

366 B.C.
First plebeian
elected to office
of consul

287 B.C.
Full equality
between
patricians and
plebeians

471 B.C.
Plebeians choose
their own tribune

445 B.C.
Marriage between
patricians and
plebeians allowed

The Roman Republic

Here's how the republic was to work: Instead of one king ruling for life, the patricians would select two *consuls* and give them *imperium*, which means kingly power. Their imperium had a few limits, however.

First, was a term limit: consuls ruled for only one year.

Second, each consul could veto the other's decision (veto means "I forbid" in Latin). This rule encouraged the consuls to get along.

Third, the consuls had to follow the rule of *consilium*, meaning that they *had to consult* with the patricians about important decisions.

When their terms were up, ex-consuls rejoined the patricians in a group called the *Senate*, where they all ruled as equals, called *senators*. Not bad for a new form of government (but it eventually gets even better)!

This concept map shows how the republic worked:

The Republic

The republic opened a door to the future. All of these modern countries have modern republics, partly inspired by the Romans: France, Italy, Mexico, and the United States. (That's got to count as proof of history's importance!)

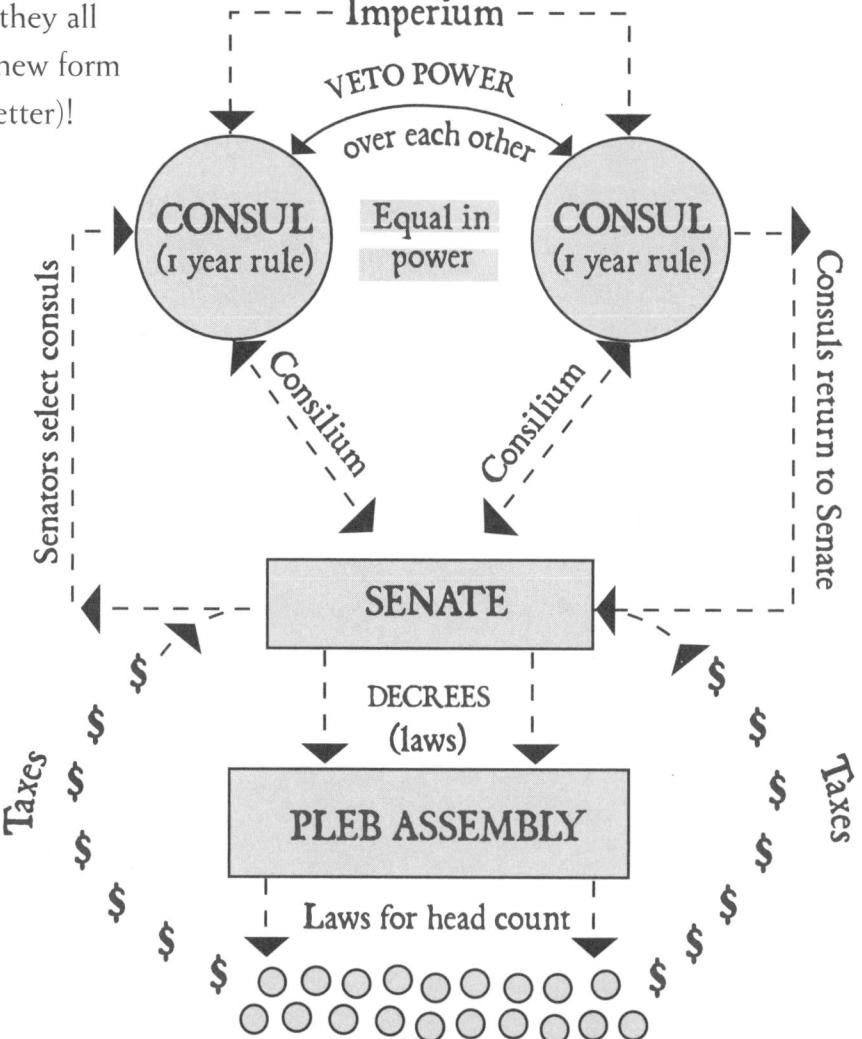

Set Up a Senate

Is there a problem or challenge facing your school or family? Then, become a "wise one" and set up a senate. You and your friends or family can create ideas and give advice about how the problem should be handled. To play the part of senators, think about a question that affects the group, such as "How can we help out if Mom loses her job?" or "What should the school do about cheaters?"

Following the Roman example, the oldest person opens and closes the senate meeting. Then, one by one, everyone gets an opportunity to offer ideas and suggestions, without any interruption. (One to three minutes of speaking for each person is usually a good amount of time.) Senators are expected to offer reasons about *why* they think as they do.

After each senator has spoken, they all discuss the different ideas and try to reach an agreement, which is written up as a decree. In Roman tradition you would then say,

"It pleases us to advise that (for example) if Mom loses her job the family should help out in the following ways:

1. Each of us gets an after-school or weekend job, giving two-thirds of our pay toward the family's expenses.

2. Stop our allowances for the time being.

3. Bring lunch to school instead of buying it.

4. Make gifts instead of buying them.

5. Not complain to Mom about not having enough money."

Worldly Words

CONSULS AND SENATORS

No doubt you see lots of links to the word *consul*, which is from the Latin word *consulere*, meaning "to consult." In Latin, the word *senator* means "elder" or "old guy." (The Latin *senex* means "older.") The senators and consuls were revered for their wisdom, and wore special gold rings and metal spurs on their boots.

The United States Government

Like Rome's, the United States' government is a republic, where citizens vote for other citizens who represent them in the government.

Unlike Rome, the United States is a *democracy*, too. That means that in the U.S. each citizen over the age of 18 — rich or poor, male or female, of any race, religion, or sexual orientation — has the right to vote. In Rome, only men had the right to vote and only landowners could serve in the Senate.

But did you know that in the beginning of the United States only certain male property owners had the right to vote? The "founding fathers" followed Roman ways when they made those rules! Eventually, by giving women and others the right to full citizenship, including the right to vote, the United States moved away from Roman values, toward a true democracy.

Try It! Make a difference. The only way a democracy can really work is if those who have a right to vote actually *do* vote. (Only 51 percent of eligible voters voted in the last presidential election.) You can make a difference even if you are not old enough to vote. Talk to the adults in your life and urge them to learn about the issues and the candidates. Then, encourage them to vote. Ask them to bring you to the polls on Election Day. That'll get them there!

P.S. If you know people eligible for U.S. citizenship who have not become citizens, help them study for the exams so they can become citizens and participate in democracy.

The Orders of Roman People

The Romans lived in a world of orders, or classes, in their new republic. That meant people were above or below other people, and those above could order those below around!

Here are the orders — in order — from most to least powerful:

▨ **Patricians** were the absolute top of society. Some even claimed that their ancestors were gods! In early Rome, it was against the law for a patrician to work at any business, except farming.

▨ **Plebeians,** or *plebs* (the everyday people) were all the other Roman citizens, including the **equestrians** (who were knights and businessmen). The *plebs* paid taxes and fought as soldiers, just as the patricians did. But they had far fewer rights in the beginning of the republic. This unfairness led to the *Struggle of the Orders* (page 46) and the creation of a three-part government.

How Many More Kinds of ORDER Can You Think of?

The word order has its roots in French, which is one of the Romance languages. What do these uses have in common? How many more can you and your friends think up in five minutes?

- ORDER in the court!
- Please get your room in ORDER, before we leave!
- May I take your ORDER?
- Please line up in alphabetical ORDER.
- The Romans had people "pigeon-holed" in ORDERS.
- Follow my ORDERS ... pul-eeze!
- In biology class, we learned about genus, species, class, ORDER, and family.
- Is your phone out of ORDER?
- Phew! All of that yard work was a tall ORDER for one afternoon.

▨ **Freemen,** including freed slaves, were sometimes called the "head count." Not very flattering — but much worse, it tells you a lot about how the orders resulted in the poor treatment of many people. Freemen did not own land or hold government positions.

▨ **Slaves,** the lowest order, were captured in conquered lands or born to other slaves. Some, like Greek slaves, became nannies or respected teachers, but most led miserable lives, under horrible conditions (see SPARTACUS, page 83).

Because of money, war, marriage, or luck, people would occasionally rise or fall from an order, but most stayed in one place for life. Not surprisingly, people in the higher orders liked this system much more than those in lower ones!

The Struggle of the Orders

Have you ever formed a club? Or been left out of one? Then you have something in common with ancient Romans. They had all kinds of exclusive groups — and the patricians, who were the senators, were the most exclusive of all. They had *all* the power and made *all* the rules — in government, religion, and the military. (If a member of the *plebs* owed a patrician a debt, like a bag of seeds, the patrician could legally declare the plebeian a slave.)

In time, some *plebs* became as wealthy as patricians. They felt they should be treated as equals. They wanted one plebeian in the Senate. The patricians said, "No!"

They asked that plebeian-patrician marriages be legalized. And some *plebs* wanted to help the poor. The patricians said, "No!" again.

That set the frustrated *plebs* into action. Riding on horseback to a nearby hill, they proclaimed a new plebeian government. With that, the worried patricians quickly promised to write new laws. They allowed the *plebs* to form their own assembly, with *tribunes* instead of consuls, who over time, made the laws in Rome.

This *Struggle of the Orders* — with common people struggling for their rights — took a couple of hundred years, from about 494–287 B.C. But when it was over, the *plebs* had far more power, and a "new nobility" of rich *plebs* and patricians ruled Rome.

The world's first republic government had been formed!

FRUSTRATED PLEBS

Order in the Court!

The Roman legal system was like the one used in many countries, including the United States and Canada today. It's all part of the Roman legacy. They had lawyers arguing in front of a judge and the judge making the final decision, just as we do. Many of our best legal ideas come directly from Rome.

Twelve Tables of Law

The very first Roman laws — written by patricians, of course — were called the *Twelve Tables of Law.* Notice that they were *written* so that they were not just kept in some people's heads. Writing them down made them more official. Every Roman boy had to memorize them.

You can see that patricians *insisted* upon respect from this early law from the Twelve Tables about singing:

"If any person has sung or composed a song that was causing insult to another … he should be clubbed to death."

Imagine what the Roman Senate would do to today's comedians! Ouch and double ouch!

Mac and cheese every Tuesday night?

Write Laws on a Scroll

Instead of books, the Romans usually wrote on scrolls. Pretend that *you* are a new tribune that must propose the laws that people must follow. (Remember, the laws must be voted on by the people.) What laws will *you* make for your home, school, and country?

Write four laws for each on three large pieces of paper taped together, along the narrow edge (so the scroll is long). Use Roman numerals (page 5) to number each law. When you are finished, glue chopsticks to the top and bottom. Use plenty of glue.

When dry, roll up the paper *from both ends* and tie it with ribbon. Store the scroll in a small pail, as the Romans did.

P.S. If you want your scroll to look very old, take a wet tea bag and squeeze some tea on your paper. Let it dry. Then, write your laws on it.

The Forum: Center of Ancient Rome

The Forum was the center of the Roman universe! In that open, rectangular area, Romans met their friends, shopped, read notices, voted, listened to speeches, and enjoyed festivals. Visiting the Forum was like reading a living newspaper.

Over the centuries, the Forum changed many times, and many more Forums were built. But in the hearts of all Romans, no matter where or when they lived, the first *Forum Romanum* meant home.

Here are 14 features of the first *Forum Romanum*:

1. *Lacus Curtius* (Curtian Gulf). Like the Romans themselves, the first Forum had a humble beginning — as a swamp! When the swamp was drained (or possibly after an earthquake) a deep crack, or *abyss*, appeared in the middle. The traditional story says that a soldier named Marcus Curtius offered himself as a sacrifice there, so that the gods would make Rome *eternal* (last forever)! Curtius rode his horse into the abyss, disappearing forever. People threw gifts in after him, and the abyss filled in.

2. Temple of Saturn. Saturn, god of agriculture and money, was Jupiter's father. Babies were registered as citizens at his temple, which also served as a bank. (See SATURNALIA, page 79.)

RUINS OF THE ANCIENT *FORUM ROMANUM*, ROME, ITALY

3. *Comitium.* Remember that *mundus* that Romulus's men supposedly dug (page 16)? It became the *Comitium*, a saucer-shaped area, set in a rectangle where the plebeian assembly gathered to vote. In front of it is the *Rostra*, where the speaker stands. (Recognize the words *committee* and *rostrum?*)

4. *Lapis Niger* **(Black Stone)** is a flat black stone, where Romulus supposedly left for heaven. It had a statue of a lion on it that has never been found. (How do you think we know about the statue?)

5. *Cloaca Maxima* **and the Shrine of** *Cloacina* **(Big Sewer and Big Sewer Goddess).** No kidding. The practical Romans built the sewer so large that small ships could sail on it! It had lots of water flowing all the time, so it wasn't too nasty. They built it so well that it is still used today. The shrine has Venus and Cloacina statues, holding flowers, near a pillar with a bird on top. The sewer runs under the Forum.

6. Temple of Vesta. The goddess of the hearth had a temple containing Vesta's holy fire. This hangout of the vestal virgins had beautiful gardens and little pools.

7. *Regia.* This is the triangular palace where kings, and later, the head priest lived. The head priest was called the *pontifex maximus,* which means "best bridge builder."

8. Temple of Castor and Pollux. This temple for Jupiter's twin sons was built to celebrate Rome's victory over the Latins.

9. *Curia Hostilia* (Hostilius's Senate House). The Senate's first meeting place, built by King Hostilius, the *Curia* overlooked the *Comitium.* That way, the senators could "look down" on the plebeians and see how they voted.

10. *Carcer.* This prison, once a water well, was where people were *incarcerated* while on trial. (Under it was the *Tullianum,* a dungeon. You don't want to know what went on *there.*)

11. Temple of Concord. In Latin, *con* means "with" and *cordia* means "heart." The name makes perfect sense as it was built to commemorate the new nobility, a joining of the patricians and rich plebeians after the Struggle of the Orders (page 46).

12. Fornix. The soldiers returning from battle would supposedly be cleansed of war's brutality by walking under this arch, which was the first triumphal arch to be built in Rome (page 25).

13. Tabernae. These long wooden tables were for butchers, bankers, and merchants. During a big speech or festival, people sat on them as benches.

14. Golden Milestone. This 6-foot-high (2 m) pillar of gold marked the center of Rome. *"All roads lead to Rome"* became a saying because eventually all roads *did* lead to the golden marker.

FORUM ROMANUM, TEMPLE OF ANTONINUS AND FAUSTINA
(LEFT) AND S. COSMA AND DAMIANO CHURCH (RIGHT)

Make a Pizza-Box Forum

"Rome wasn't built in a day" is another old saying. But, if you like pizza, you and some friends can create a model of the *Forum Romanum* any day, anytime!

1. The pizza box. Paint or paper the inside of a pizza box. Decorate the lid with Roman themes or a paper mosaic (page 40). That way, your Forum will look very Roman when it's closed, too. One flap can be the *Servian Wall* built by King Servius. The other can be the *Via Sacra*, the old road that leads to the Forum.

2. Pop-ups, flaps, and creativity. Bring your Forum to life with creativity! Gather all kinds of art materials, old magazines, and air-drying clay. Paste pictures on cardboard and stick them in clay; make pillars of rolled paper.

To make pop-ups: Fold skinny strips of paper, accordion-style. Paste one end to the back of the figure, the other to the bottom of the box.

3. Buildings, temples, *tabernae* (benches), and more. Use your ingenuity, along with found materials. A ripped bottom for the Curtian Gulf? A golden toothpick stuck in clay for the Golden Milestone? A dotted line to show where the sewer was underneath the Forum? It's up to you! Be on the lookout for ideas that show the features of each place. The Temple of Saturn might have a couple of coins pasted nearby, and the Temple of Concord might have a heart. Add a lion's picture at the Black Stone. Construct the *tabernae* from brown cardboard folded into a U shape, with two rows running northeast and southwest.

4. Mark N, S, E, and W for compass points. The orderly Romans often used these four points when they built.

5. Add people from all of the orders (page 45), either using action figures or making your own figures from peanuts in their shells or using pipe cleaners, dressed in proper attire.

Highways and Waterways: The Expansion of Rome

Of all the gifts the Roman builders and engineers left us, these three stand out: great concrete buildings, sturdy roads, and magnificent Roman aqueducts. The Romans weren't brilliant inventors, but they sure knew how to improve what was already around. We already saw what they did with the arch. They improved architecture by discovering how to make vaults that were like stone arches in a ceiling. This made the inside of Roman buildings pillar-free, airy, and light. The greatest example is the Pantheon, which still stands today.

Make Cement Garden Stepping-Stones

For building, the Romans used concrete, called *pozzolana*, from crushed stone mixed with volcanic ash. What is amazing is that the volcanic ash seems to make the concrete waterproof, too. To find out how long-lasting concrete can be, create stepping-stones for a garden. (Add your own bit of history for someone else to uncover by adding your handprint and etching the date in the concrete before it dries.)

▨ **You'll need:**

Trowel

Prepared path or deep, disposable pie plate

Gravel or pebbles

Quick-setting cement (for use with
   adult help)

Water

Pail or basin for mixing

Petroleum jelly

Stick

Decorations: pebbles, shells, tiles, beads,
   dried seeds, sea glass, marbles, fake
   gems, and other favorite decorative
   items; patio or basement paint; or food
   coloring and paintbrush

PANTHEON, BUILT FROM 30 B.C.–A.D. 124, ROME, ITALY

1. Dig a hole in the garden the size and shape that you would like your stepping-stone to be and about 2" (5 cm) deep. The bottom of the hole should be smooth and level. (You can also make your stepping-stone in the pie plate.) Add about 1" (2.5 cm) of gravel or pebbles.

2. With an adult's help, follow the instructions on the bag of cement to mix it with water in the pail. Stir with the trowel. The concrete should be fairly stiff — so that a scoop of it doesn't fall off the trowel when you hold it upside down.

3. Fill the hole with concrete and smooth the surface. Let the concrete harden for about an hour.

4. Now, you're ready to decorate! To add a handprint (or footprint), cover your hand or foot with petroleum jelly (to protect your skin from the concrete) and press it into the stone (then wash up). Use a sturdy stick to write your name and the date. (If the impressions don't stay, smooth out the concrete again and let it harden longer.) Add other decorations such as pebbles or small tiles. Add color with paint or food coloring.

5. Let the stone cure for a week (cover an outdoor one with plastic if it rains) before stepping on it.

Make a Roman Highway

The first great Roman highway, the *Appian Way*, led south, to the villas of wealthy Romans. As Rome expanded, more highways were built to link all the parts of the far-flung lands together. The Romans built 53 *million* miles of roads!

▨ You'll need:

Piece of shallow pottery or an aluminum
   baking dish, at least 10" (25 cm) wide
Soil
4 toothpicks
String
Teaspoon
Small decorative stones (glass aquarium
   stones are good)
Pebbles, sand, gravel (for the "hard core")
Larger stones
Baby plants or grass seed
Water

APPIAN WAY WITH ORIGINAL COBBLESTONES,
OUTSIDE ROME, ITALY

**Follow the basic process
that Roman engineers used:**

1. Fill the dish with soil; press it down.

2. Mark the line of the road, by planting two toothpicks on each side of the road ends (use four toothpicks in all). The toothpicks should be about 3"–4" (7.5–10 cm) apart for the road bed.

3. Tie string tightly to the toothpicks to make a straight guideline along the sides of the road. The Romans used the shortest route possible.

4. On the outside of each string, dig a narrow "ditch" with the end of the teaspoon. Press similar-sized decorative stones into the soil along the sides.

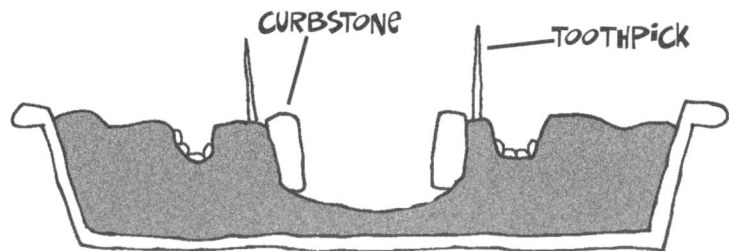

5. On the inside of the toothpicks, dig out a roadbed. Press similar-sized large stones into the soil along the sides for curbstones.

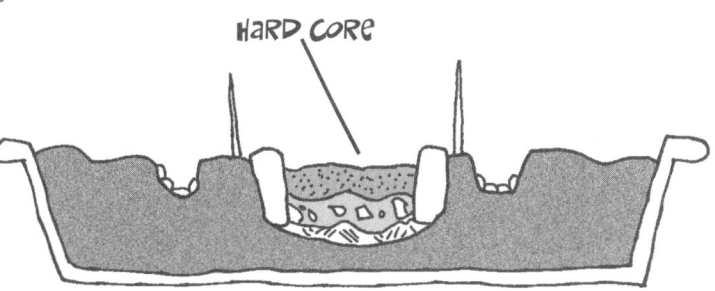

6. Fill the scooped-out road with the *hard core* — different layers of pebbles, sand, and gravel.

7. For the top layer, add larger stones, highest in the middle so that the road gently slopes at each side for good drainage into the side ditches, as the Romans did.

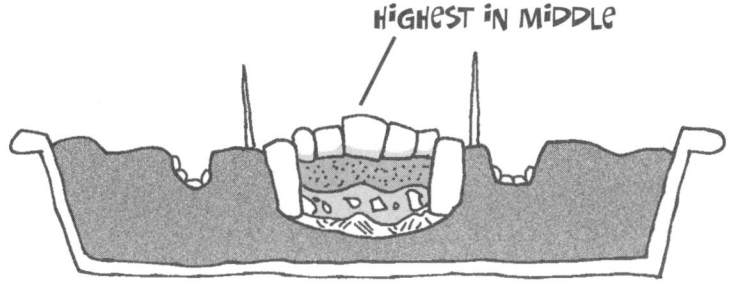

8. Plant grass seed or small plants in the soil, along the edges. Water as needed.

For a final touch, put some horses and people on your Roman road. The road should survive many rainstorms (when you water your plants) and last for *centuries!*

Build a Roman Aqueduct

Water, water, everywhere — but not in the middle of a city! When cities need water, it usually needs to be piped in from faraway. Using the force of gravity, the Romans channeled mountain water slowly downhill through magnificent structures called *aqueducts*.

▦ **You'll need:** large cereal box, scissors or craft knife (use only with adult supervision), pencil, ruler, lightweight cardboard, compass (or can), stapler, tacky glue, 16" square (40 cm) of heavy-weight cardboard, paper-towel tube, plastic garbage bag, container (or small plant), water

AN ANCIENT ROMAN AQUEDUCT, BUILT A.D. 89–117, SEGOVIA, SPAIN

1. Cut off the top, bottom, and one side of the cereal box. Draw a line down the middle of the remaining side and cut along this line.

2. To make the bridge: Place one of the pieces, printed side *down*, and draw one half of a bridge 12" (30 cm) long, making it 8" (20 cm) tall at one end and slanting it down to 6½" (16 cm) at the other end. Repeat with the second piece, placing it printed side *up*.

8"(20 cm)

6½" (16 cm)

12"(30 cm)

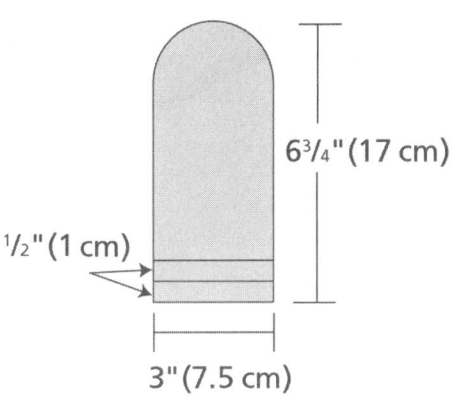

6³/₄" (17 cm)

¹/₂" (1 cm)

3" (7.5 cm)

3. Make an arch template from the light-weight cardboard by drawing a rectangle 3" x 6 ³/₄" (7.5 x 17 cm) and rounding the corners using the compass (or the can). Cut out the template and draw two lines across the bottom, each ¹/₂" (1 cm) above the last.

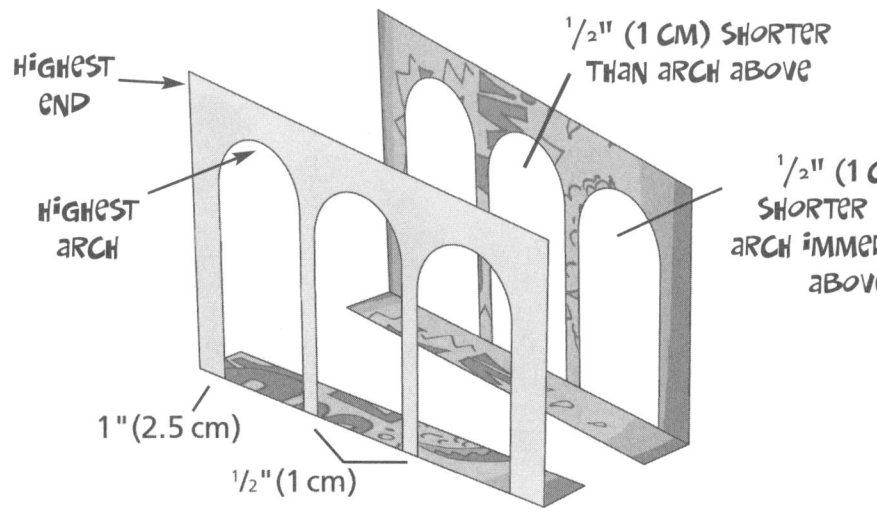

HiGHEST END

HiGHEST aRCH

¹/₂" (1 CM) SHORTER THAN aRCH aBove

¹/₂" (1 CM) SHORTER THAN aRCH iMMeDiaTeLy aBove

1" (2.5 cm)

¹/₂" (1 cm)

4. To make the arches: Using your template, draw three arches on each of the bridge halves, ¹/₂" (1 cm) apart, starting 1" (2.5 cm) in from the highest end. Using the lines on the bottom of the template, make each arch ¹/₂" (1 cm) shorter than the last. Cut out the arches, without cutting out the stand.

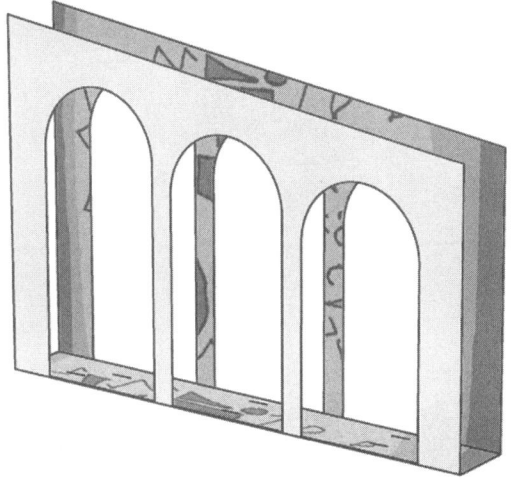

5. Overlap the two bridge halves and staple the bottoms together. Glue the bridge to the heavy cardboard for support. Let dry.

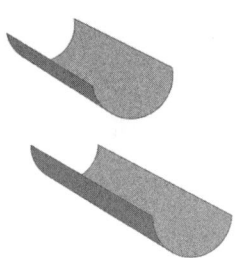
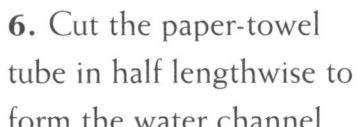

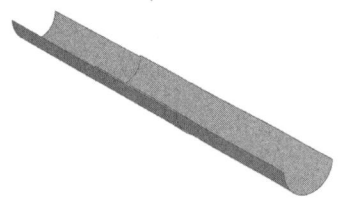

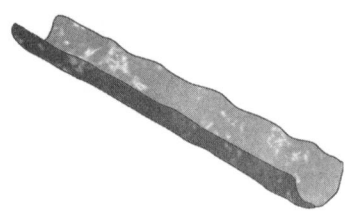

6. Cut the paper-towel tube in half lengthwise to form the water channel.

The channel should be 2" (5 cm) longer than the bridges, so glue the two half-tubes together.

Cut a piece of the garbage bag to fit; glue it to cover the channel, smoothing it as you glue. Let dry.

7. Assembling the aqueduct: Glue the sides of the channel to the top insides of the bridge with the extra length of the channel sticking out at the lower end.

8. Place the container (or a small plant) at the lower end of the aqueduct as you pour water at the higher end of your channel.

Nice job! You've built a replica of an aqueduct (that works equally well for watering plants or rolling marbles into a bucket!).

Looking Ahead

We've traveled a long way through time in our imaginary parade, but there's no stopping now. We've seen Rome rise from a grassy hill to a great city and progress from a kingdom to a self-governing republic. But look ahead. It appears that there are soldiers, weary from war, marching in the parade.

Conquest, Conflict & the End of the Republic

"There was nothing that did more to advance the greatness of the Romans than that she did always unite and incorporate those whom she conquered into herself."

—PLUTARCH, GREEK HISTORIAN

So many *soldiers!* And after them, fabulous floats of treasure! It's a *triumph* with Romans celebrating victory over other lands! But wait, is that cheering or jeering? Is the parade of Roman history taking a nasty turn?

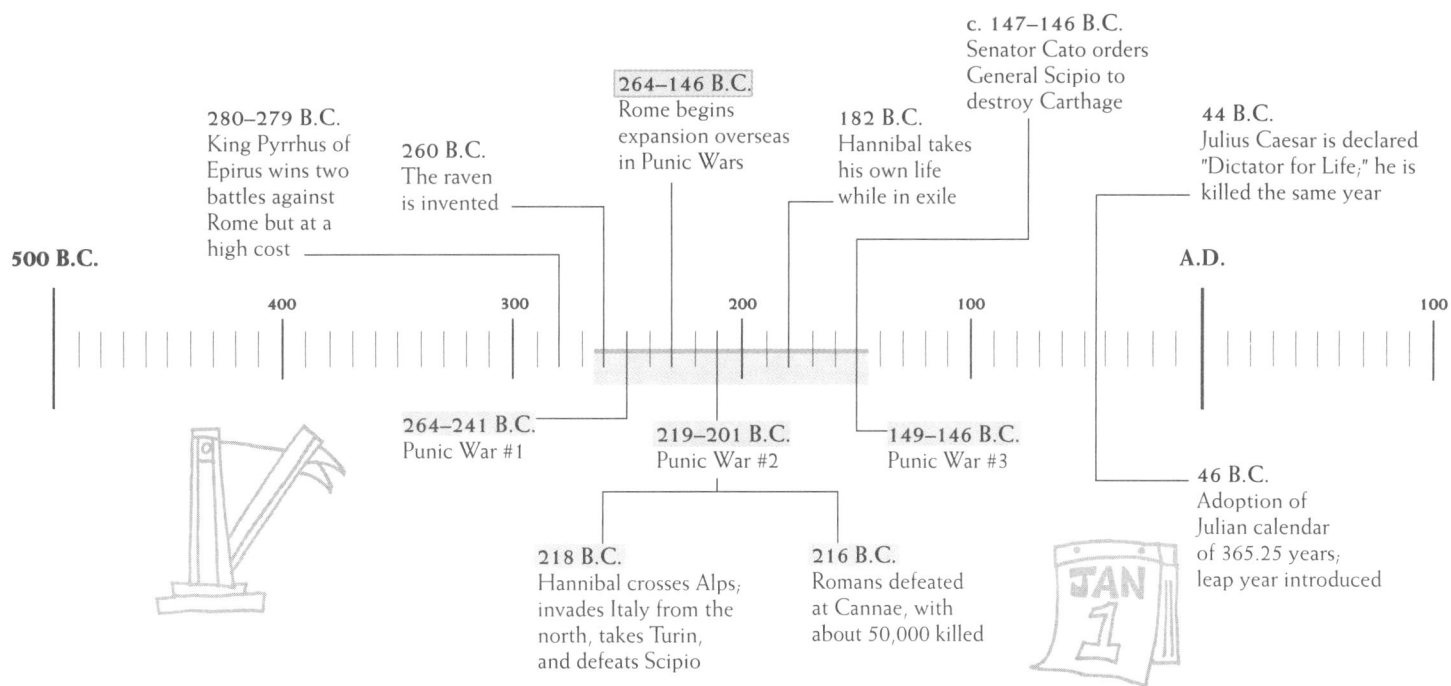

c. 147–146 B.C.
Senator Cato orders General Scipio to destroy Carthage

280–279 B.C.
King Pyrrhus of Epirus wins two battles against Rome but at a high cost

260 B.C.
The raven is invented

264–146 B.C.
Rome begins expansion overseas in Punic Wars

182 B.C.
Hannibal takes his own life while in exile

44 B.C.
Julius Caesar is declared "Dictator for Life;" he is killed the same year

500 B.C.

400

300

200

A.D.

100

100

264–241 B.C.
Punic War #1

219–201 B.C.
Punic War #2

149–146 B.C.
Punic War #3

218 B.C.
Hannibal crosses Alps; invades Italy from the north, takes Turin, and defeats Scipio

216 B.C.
Romans defeated at Cannae, with about 50,000 killed

46 B.C.
Adoption of Julian calendar of 365.25 years; leap year introduced

A Time of Growth and Conquest

It took the Romans hundreds of years to gain control of central Italy, but only 50 years to take over the entire Mediterranean world! How did they pull that off, friend? Think about the early clue about the two sides of Roman nature (page 6). Well, even the Roman conquests had two faces: force and friendship. And let's not forget that where there is force, there is bloodshed and disruption of people's lives.

Here is the basic — and brilliant — plan that won the world for Rome:

1. **Team up** with friends to make a big army to defeat the enemy.

2. **Promise** the defeated leaders that they can live in peace and worship as they please — as long as they send soldiers and pay taxes to the Romans.

3. **Give** the defeated leaders and their families the gift of Roman citizenship.

Success for the Romans! The conquered land was now part of the growing empire.

Drama of the Battlefield

The trumpets blast! The *standards* (royal emblems) are lifted! The Romans are ready for conquest! And the Romans' love of the military certainly is evident throughout their history. Whenever the army of young soldiers rode into battle, rising over everything was an *aquila*, or eagle — the symbol of Roman power that was carried by a soldier on horseback. How their enemies must have feared that sight!

Try It! To make an aquila, you'll need silver poster board (or white, painted silver), a black marker, scissors, a ballpoint pen, string, and an old broom.

Draw an eagle with its wings spread across the poster board, making it as big as the poster board to impress the enemy. Cut it out.

Punch two holes with the ballpoint pen in the middle of the eagle, lengthwise, about 4" (10 cm) apart. Thread the holes with string, and tie the string around the broom bristles.

You are now ready to lead the troops into battle!

To suffer hardness with good cheer,
In sternest school of warfare bred,
Our youth should learn. Let horse and spear
Make him one day the enemy's dread.

—HORACE, "THE DUTIES OF YOUTH"

Heading into Battle

Imagine being a typical soldier in the well-organized Roman army. You'd be disciplined, obedient, faithful, and industrious — ready to answer the trumpet's call to arms.

On your waist is a sword. In your hand, is a *javelin*, a long stick with an arrowlike end. You have a 60-pound (27 kg) pack, full of tools, because you have been trained to build as well as to fight. You also carry a water bag, cooking tools, clothes, and your personal possessions from a pole. The goatskin that covers the shield on your back will be your blanket tonight.

Each day you march for hours, but that's not hard for you. Back home, you trained and practiced every day to get strong. The dummy weapons you trained with were *twice* as heavy as the real ones you carry now. Yes, you were well prepared.

Try It! Will *your* body respond to training? Find out! Look for a safe place (like your local high school track) and time (daylight) to run. Note the time and then run until you get *winded* (out of breath). Note the time again. How long could you run? Then, every day for the next three weeks faithfully practice running in place, running at the track, or doing daily jumping jacks. After three weeks, return to the track and time yourself again. How much longer can you run now?

Clash of Titans: Rome vs. Carthage

The Romans' fiercest rivals were the descendants of the sea-faring *Phoenicians*, the *Carthaginians*. They lived in Africa in the city of Carthage and on the islands off Italy.

Today, powerful nations try to work together. But in ancient times, that possibility was still undiscovered. Back then, only *one* power could rule. Would it be Rome or Carthage?

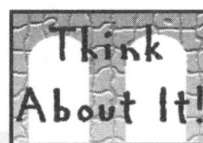

Patriotism and the Roman Legacy

It feels good to be part of your country in a positive way. But what if your country takes actions you disagree with? This happened in the United States during the Vietnam War.

Many Americans who opposed the war had meetings, protests, and wrote songs against it. Critics called them unpatriotic and told them to support their country "right or wrong."

Others felt that their protests were what freedom of speech is all about: We all should have the right to express our opinions — even in times of war!

In Roman times, patriotism meant supporting the men who were in charge — no matter what! Today, patriotism means loving your country.

But loving a nation and being completely uncritical of it are different. (After all, the adults in your life may love you very much, but we bet they are critical of some things you do!) Blind loyalty to anything or anyone can lead to very bad situations.

Then, September 11, 2001 happened. Patriotism and love of world freedom became extremely important to people around the globe. If you never asked yourself before, now is a good time to ask, "What does patriotism mean to me?"

A Great Naval Power: Punic War #1

Carthage had a powerful navy, and the Romans had practically none. But instead of worrying, the Romans got to work. They found a Carthaginian ship and made 120 copies of it in six weeks! As the ships were being made, soldiers sat on benches practicing rowing, hour after hour.

The Romans also added a new and deadly feature to the ships — a swiveling plank with a spike on the end (that attached like a bridge to the enemy ship), called the *raven*. Instead of ramming an enemy ship to sink it, as was done in those days, the Romans used the raven, crossed it to the other ship, and battled in the way they knew best, as if on land.

So much for Carthage's superior navy!

Hannibal and Punic War #2

Hannibal was the Romans' toughest foe. As a boy, he had promised the gods of Carthage that he would never be a friend to the Romans — and, oh, how he kept that promise!

He launched one of the great sneak attacks in history by entering Italy from the north, climbing the ice-covered Alps with 40,000 men and 60 elephants! In another battle at Cannae, his soldiers killed 50,000 Romans *in one day!*

Still, the Romans refused to give up.

Hannibal stayed in Italy for 12 years, making trouble for the Romans and trying to get the other Italians to turn against them. But like the Sabine women of old (page 23), the Italian allies had grown comfortable with their conquerors. Hannibal was a defeated man who had "won the battle, but lost the war."

"I Don't Know How — But I'd Sure Like to Learn!"

Does the story of the Roman navy sound like powerful Roman determination? The Romans weren't necessarily good at everything or even great at anything, but they weren't too proud to learn from those who knew something they didn't know! Have you ever used that same trait to improve yourself? How'd it work out for you?

Hannibal's Genius

Hannibal came up with ideas in a way that is sometimes called "thinking outside the box." He did not limit ideas to the tried-and-true; his ideas were *untried* and *new!* Here is an example of one of his surprise tactics: In ancient times, men fought in rows. Most generals put the strongest soldiers front and center and the weakest ones, on the sides and in back. Hannibal did the opposite. He put the weakest in the center and strongest on the sides and in back.

When the rows met, the enemy smashed through the middle of the front line — only to find themselves caught, as if in a net!

Try It! Get some pennies and dimes and re-create Hannibal's tactic. Use double-stacked coins for the strong soldiers and single coins for weaker ones. Arrange the coins in three tight rows of four across for each "army." Then, let the battle begin! Move the coins toward each other. When a "strong" one has contact with a "weak" one, eliminate the weak one. (Thank goodness coins don't bleed!)

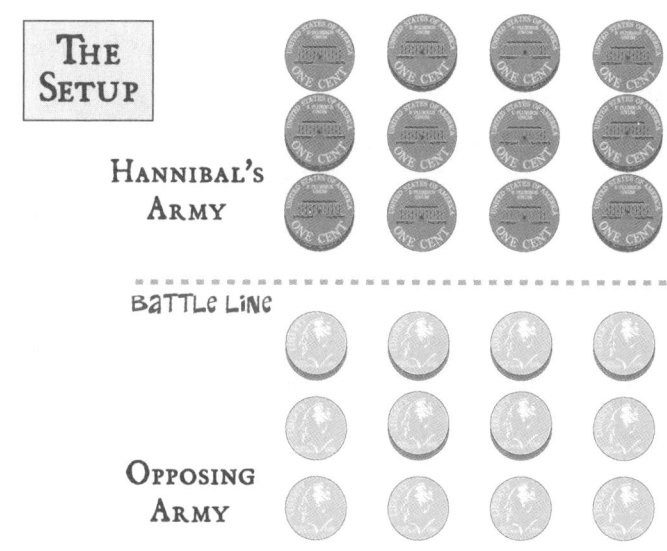

THE SETUP

HANNIBAL'S ARMY

BATTLE LINE

OPPOSING ARMY

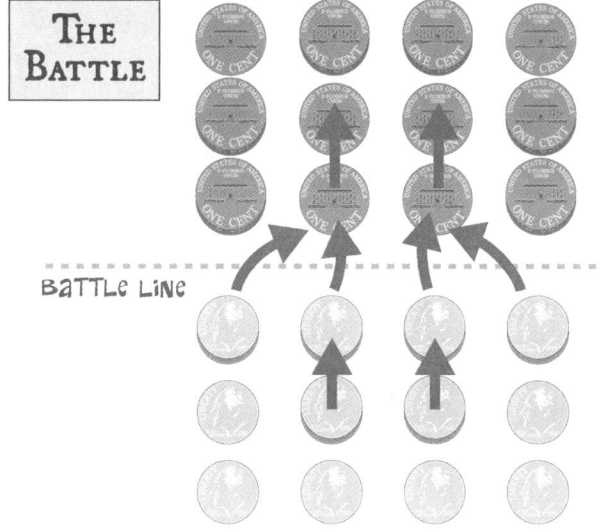

THE BATTLE

BATTLE LINE

THE OPPOSING ARMY ADVANCES.
STRONG SOLDIERS ATTACK WEAK ONES.

THE RESULT

THE STRONG SOLDIERS OF THE OPPOSING ARMY ARE NOW CAUGHT IN A "NET." PLUS, THEY ARE MORE TIRED THAN HANNIBALS'S BACKLINE SOLDIERS.

Punic War #3:
Destruction and a Shameful Turn

The Romans took half of Spain from the Carthaginians and then smashed their way southward. Finally, the Senate led by Senator *Cato* ordered Roman *General Scipio* to destroy Carthage. As flames engulfed the great city, the great General Scipio cried. He realized that the Roman action was too harsh and not in the Roman style of preserving the ways of captured cultures and lands.

Archaeologists today call this action Rome's great shame. Because they desired revenge, a magnificent city was wiped off the face of the earth, leaving nothing for history!

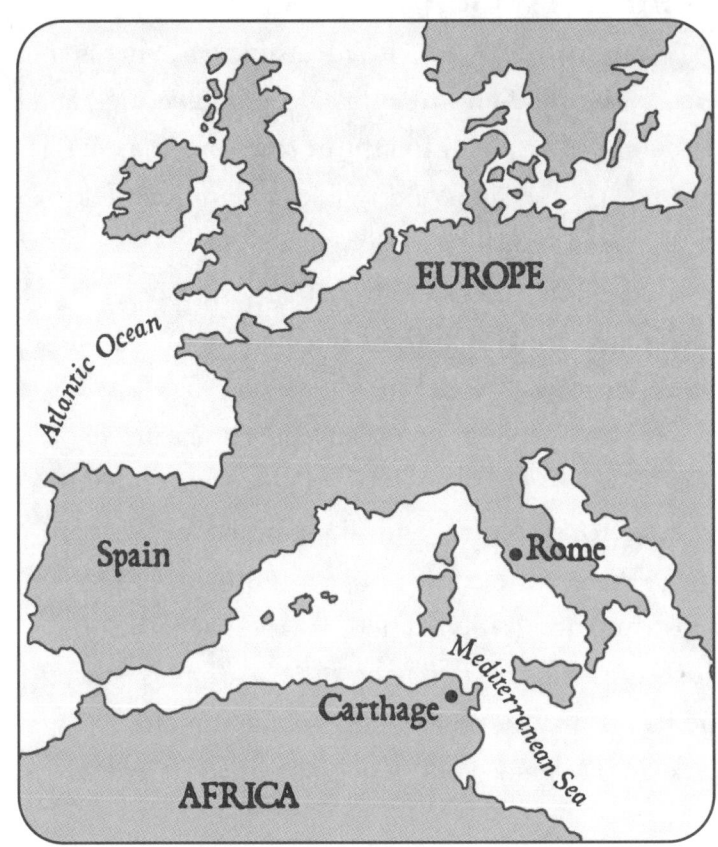

Worldly Words

A Pyrrhic Victory

When the Romans had taken over central Italy and were looking southward, the Greeks who lived in the south asked *King Pyrrhus* of Epirus to defend them. He sailed to Italy with 40,000 soldiers and beat the Romans, *twice*. But the Romans refused to give up! They defeated Pyrrhus in a third battle, and he finally went home, leaving Rome in charge.

When congratulated on his first victories, Pyrrhus supposedly murmured, "More victories like that and I am finished!" Since then, the expression *pyrrhic* (peer-IK) *victory* has meant "empty victory" — a battle won at too high a cost.

You have probably experienced a pyrrhic victory of your own. Maybe you and a friend argued, and though you got the last word in, the friendship was lost. There you have it — a pyrrhic victory, which isn't a victory at all.

Enter Julius Caesar

As conflicts raged, a patrician *Populare* (page 68) named *Julius Caesar* stepped forward to help Rome. He was an outstanding military leader who conquered Gaul and won the loyalty of his soldiers. He was a good governor who ran the new lands efficiently, too.

Instead of plotting against his political opponents, he *forgave* them — a first for Rome! People of the time wrote that he was kind, intelligent, funny, and generous, even if he did like to show off. Most Romans loved him — despite his breaking traditions!

After he was elected consul, his friends in the Senate let him do what he wanted. He liked to wear the purple toga of triumph, so they let him. He liked sitting on a gold throne, so they got him one. He liked to rule, so they said he could be dictator for life! All that Caesar needed to become king was a golden crown — so they offered him one!

Caesar refused the crown, but that did not satisfy a few *Optimates* (page 68) who resented his *popularity* (notice anything about that word?). Those *Optimates* did not want Rome to return to the rule of kings.

Now what?

Worldly Words

COMPLETELY CRASSUS

The word *crass,* meaning "crude" or "insensitive," comes from a rich Roman named *Crassus,* who owned a private fire company. When a fire blazed, he would show up and demand high fees to put it out! Of course, desperate customers offered him *anything* — even their lives as slaves — to save their homes! If it burned, he showed up afterward and bought up the property cheap! Then he rebuilt and rented at high rates. Can you imagine?

As a general battling Spartacus's slave rebellion (page 83), Crassus told his soldiers that if they didn't win, he would have them killed! Treating people badly was just fine with Crassus — who was "soooo" crass!

Conservatives and Liberals

In every society, you can be sure there will be politicians — and that they will disagree. That's because they usually represent people who hold opposing views, often representing the *conservative* or *liberal* point of view.

Conservatism: Wanting to preserve what is already established (continue doing things the same or "old" way)

Liberalism: Wanting progress, reform, or change to protect human rights and civil liberties

In Rome, the *Optimates* were the conservatives, wanting to keep Rome as it had been, with rich patricians in control. The *Populares* (the liberals) wanted to spread the wealth, give land to landless soldiers, and give all Italians Roman citizenship.

A fierce competition broke out between the two groups. It got so bad that supposedly dignified *Optimates* threw buckets of cow dung at the *Populares!* Gangs roamed the streets of Rome and some *Populares* were murdered.

Conservatives and liberals still disagree — sometimes strongly! But at least they *try* to work together for the public good.

Caesar's To-Do List

Julius Caesar was a "take charge" kind of guy who seemed to enjoy life immensely! Here are his goals for the year 45 B.C. with a check after everything he was able to accomplish:

To-Do List

- Pardon my political enemies ✓
- Increase the number of senators ✓
- Make new laws so that the truly needy get food ✓
- Fix the calendar ✓
- Improve the port of Ostia ✓
- Direct the building of new Roman cities ✓
- Build a new Forum and name it after me
- Create a library of Greek and Roman books
- Build new roads and canals in the provinces ✓

Try It! Caesar had big dreams, but to make them come true, he had to work on them day by day, just like everybody else. Have you ever made a to-do list to help yourself to focus on what has to get done? Try it for a couple of weeks to see if it really works. And don't forget to check off what you complete!

Plus, Caesar Could Write!

In addition to all his other abilities, Caesar was a clear and *concise* (brief) writer who wrote quickly and effortlessly. One of his most famous letters was only three words long. His letter to the Senate, written after he conquered Asia Minor, said,

> ## "Veni, vidi, vici."
> ### (I came, I saw, I conquered.)

That said it all!

Keep a *Commentarii Dierum*

Caesar wrote his journal *Commentarii Dierum*, or Commentary of the Day, on wax tablets — thin layers of wax on "pages" of wood. You can write yours in a collage-covered journal.

Try It! To make a collage on a notebook cover, just arrange lots of overlapping pictures and decorative papers. Use watered-down glue to paste them on the notebook and then after they dry, paste over everything with the watered-down glue, too. Let dry.

Inside, enter the date and your thoughts, feelings, actions, hopes, and dreams. Write about any obstacles that you overcame, too. Don't be shy about giving yourself credit, either. Caesar lived *con fides* — with faith — or as we say today (thanks to the Romans), he had *confidence* in himself. So, review your day with confidence!

Great, Great, Great History for Rent

The story of the *great* Caesar was adapted by the *great* English writer, William Shakespeare! His play, *Julius Caesar* became a *great* movie starring *great* actors. Check it out, because it really is *GREAT!*

Time Changes

THE JULIAN CALENDAR

Leap year (when we add February 29th to our calendar every four years) was Julius Caesar's idea! He hated inefficiency, so he changed the entire calendar to make it more accurate. Numa's calendar (page 37) had been based on 12 moon months, which made for extra months every so often.

The Senate was so grateful to Julius Caesar that it named the month of July after him.

A Sudden End

On March 14, 44 B.C., Caesar was with friends, when the talk turned to death. A friend asked, "What kind of death is best?" Caesar replied, "That which is least expected." By that definition, Caesar had a good death.

The next day, Caesar's wife begged him to stay home from work because she had had a bad dream about the Senate. But Caesar did not pay attention to the dream. He also ignored an old man on the steps at the Forum who called out, "Caesar, beware the Ides of March!" (The Ides of March is March 15.)

JULIUS CAESAR PROCEEDING TO THE SENATE ON MARCH 15, 44 B.C.; ABEL DE PUJOL, A.D. 1857–1945

In the Senate, a few *Optimates* walked up to Caesar, pulled daggers from their togas, and stabbed him to death! One of the assassins was *Brutus*, whom Caesar had once saved from death. Shocked, Caesar supposedly uttered, *"Et tu, Brute?"* ("And you, Brutus?") Then he slumped lifelessly to the Senate floor.

The Roman people were stunned by the murder. They silently filled the Forum, where the *Optimates* tried to convince them that Caesar *deserved* to die because he wanted to be king.

Then Caesar's will was read. To every Roman citizen he left money, as well as his beautiful gardens for all to enjoy. Even in death, he was generous! But the biggest surprise was that he had adopted his 18-year-old grandnephew *Gaius Octavius* as his son and heir.

Julius Caesar had his life cut short. But this son, best known as *Octavian*, would continue in his path, opening a new chapter of Roman history, imperial Rome! And that may be the most fun part of the parade to participate in, so come along!

Life under the Emperors

Like a second Romulus, Octavian began creating a *new* Rome. He built a new forum and rebuilt the old one, made new roads and fixed old ones. He organized police and fire-fighting services, issued coins, and built new temples. And whatever he did for the city of Rome, he also did in the conquered lands, called *provinces*.

Changing his name (again!) to *Augustus*, meaning *majestic*, he created a new Roman government, ruled by just one powerful person — an emperor!

The glory days of the Roman Empire had arrived!

Augustus's Principate

Augustus Caesar's new government was called The Principate. Breaking tradition, he hired capable *plebs*, freemen, and educated slaves to run the government. He cleverly called them his "household help" to keep snobby or lazy patricians away from government work.

The Senate still met and voted, but Augustus was in complete control. He was said to "rule with a nod of his head."

P.S. Those Principate workers were the world's first "civil servants," people who are paid to run the government, day by day.

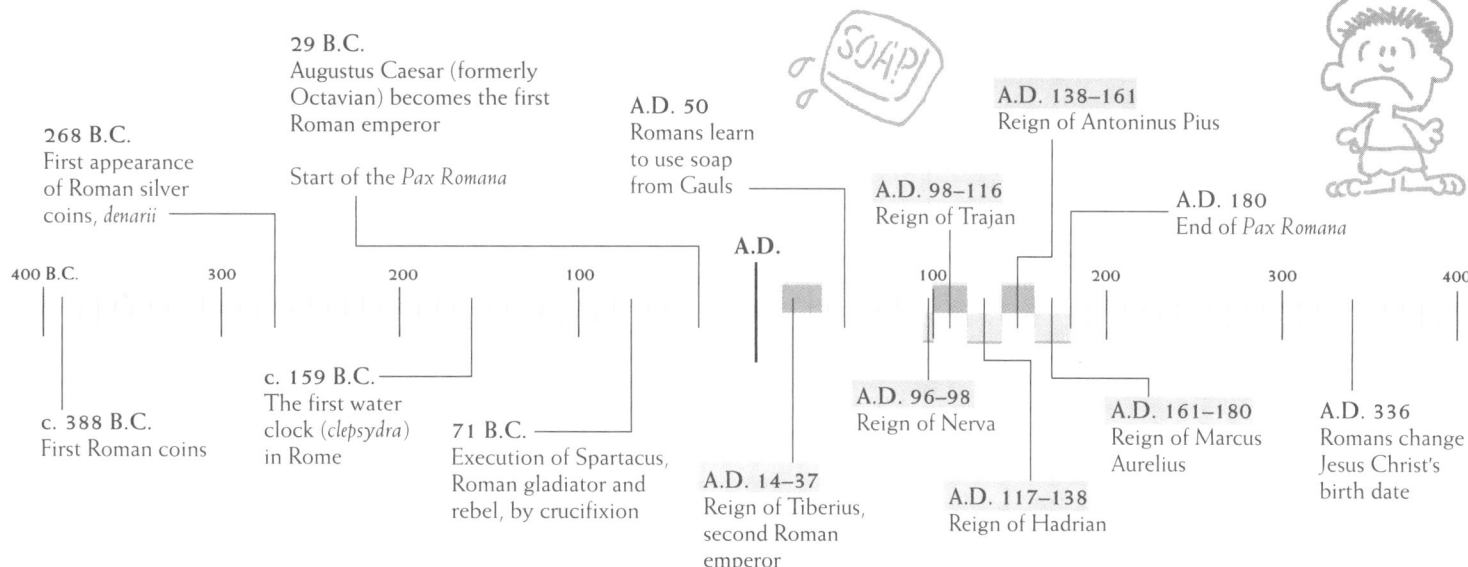

268 B.C.
First appearance of Roman silver coins, *denarii*

29 B.C.
Augustus Caesar (formerly Octavian) becomes the first Roman emperor

Start of the *Pax Romana*

A.D. 50
Romans learn to use soap from Gauls

A.D. 98–116
Reign of Trajan

A.D. 138–161
Reign of Antoninus Pius

A.D. 180
End of *Pax Romana*

400 B.C.   300   200   100   A.D.   100   200   300   400

c. 388 B.C.
First Roman coins

c. 159 B.C.
The first water clock (*clepsydra*) in Rome

71 B.C.
Execution of Spartacus, Roman gladiator and rebel, by crucifixion

A.D. 14–37
Reign of Tiberius, second Roman emperor

A.D. 96–98
Reign of Nerva

A.D. 117–138
Reign of Hadrian

A.D. 161–180
Reign of Marcus Aurelius

A.D. 336
Romans change Jesus Christ's birth date

The *Pax Romana:* One World under Rome

For about two hundred years, Rome ruled the world. This golden time, called the *Pax Romana,* or the "Peace of Rome," began with Augustus and continued under the next 14 emperors.

Even though there were more and more Roman citizens, few went hungry. Roman laws gave the people in the provinces rights and protection. Instead of Rome ruling *over* them, the conquered lands had become a mosaic of Roman provinces, where most people lived in peace, as Romans.

Treasures Galore!

Times were good! Rome had all the treasures and harvests of Egypt. It had gold and copper from Spain. It had furniture decorated with bronze, rare glass, and silks from Asia. It had spices, pearls, and gems from India, and thick carpets and perfumes from Arabia. From Greece arrived fine fabrics and marble. Gaul and the lands of Europe provided pottery, amber, iron, and tin.

But getting those goods around the Roman world took money — something else the wealthy imperial Romans had plenty of!

Coins of the Realm

Gone were the days when Roman money came in the form of trading chickens or cows. The Romans needed money that could travel around the empire. Augustus gave coins a fixed value, which greatly simplified trade.

Each coin was free advertising for the leader who issued it, too! Slogans were put on coins to remind people of the ideals and virtues of their leaders. Here's how some people spent their *denarii* during the *Pax Romana:*

Pater! I need 300 denarii for some sports sandals!

1 egg = 1 denarius

1 live chicken = 30 denarii

shoes = 100 denarii

The Rich and the Poor

According to a Roman census taken in the year A.D. 400, there were 1,750 private homes and about 44,000 apartments in the city of Rome. Those facts offer a clue to how many rich and how many everyday Romans there were at that time. Clearly, the wealth of Rome in the *Pax Romana* remained in the hands of very few.

Wealthy Romans had city town-houses and country homes called *villas* that were roomy and comfortable. In winter, outside fire pits sent steam heat behind the walls for heating.

Colorful paintings called *murals* decorated their walls. The floors had a Roman creation, *mosaics*, which are pictures or designs made from colored stones or tiles. Yes, the rich enjoyed a very elegant life, often trying to imitate the Greeks in collecting art.

Poor Romans lived in four- or five-story buildings called *insulae* that were owned by rich Romans. *Insulae* had no running water on the upper floors and were, therefore, in constant danger of fires. Several emperors declared it illegal to cook in them, which led to a Roman creation that is a big part of the world today: fast food!

Fast-food places were called *popinae*. In Rome alone, there were about 10,000 of them!

RUINS OF APARTMENT BUILDINGS IN ANCIENT
ROME, VIA DEI BALCONI, OSTIA, ITALY

Worldly Words

WHAT A PRINCE!
Augustus lived on the *Palatine* Hill, so rulers ever since have lived in a *palace*. And, he was the *princeps* ("first citizen"). Do you think that has anything to do with our English prince or princess? These language links are everywhere!

Pop in a Popina

Set up a *popina* and tell your friends to pop in! Make a large menu sign and hang it on the wall.

Popina foods: Italian bread, provolone cheese, figs, nuts, dates, sausage, and chicken to eat in or take out

Popina drinks: grape juice or lemonade sweetened with honey

But please note: You'll have to **SKIP THE TOMATO** — that came from the New World! And **SKIP THE PASTA** — that came from China!

AN ANCIENT ROMAN MOSAIC MADE OF TILES AT A ROMAN BATH, BATH, ENGLAND

Make a Cool Mosaic Trivet

Even poor Romans had a few nice possessions. Your *popina* can have a mosaic trivet for hot foods. To make it, you'll need 1 or 2 cups (250 to 500 ml) of air-drying clay, a rolling pin, a blunt knife, and flat glass pebbles or sea glass.

Make a ball from the clay and begin rolling it out, like pizza dough. Make sure it is twice as thick as the pebbles. Then, press pebbles close together into the clay — either in a recognizable shape (see the cover) or in a design — and let it dry.

Roman Leisure and Fun

With the huge empire supplying them with all they needed, the Romans — rich and poor alike — became experts at enjoyment (when they weren't fighting wars!). They loved food and parties; racing and gladiator games. They dressed up for the theater and shows at the *odeum* (page 77). They had dozens of holidays and festivals, and for everyday relaxation, they had the fabulous Roman baths.

Splish, Splash at the Roman Baths

The Romans were terribly shy — NOT! They had public toilets — some were "20 seaters" — and public baths! Friends met at bathhouses that were the most technologically advanced buildings of their time. Set in parks, they had music, entertainment, even libraries, along with several

RUINS OF ROMAN BATHS IN PORTUGAL

pools. One thing they *didn't* have yet was soap!

Try It! To make Roman-style aromatherapy bath oil that will have a pleasant effect on mind and body, add about 20 drops of rose or lavender fragrance essential oil to a cup (250 ml) of almond or safflower oil. Breathing the scents of rose or lavender is believed to have a positive effect on people's moods. The Romans seemed to know that instinctively! Men and women both used scented oil, which they often applied and scraped off (along with the dirt!) using a special scraper called a *stringilis*.

Apicius, Caterer to Rome's Elite

Apicius organized lavish dinner parties for his wealthy clients. For a special event, he once made a dish of camel heels and nightingale tongues! Ugh! You may enjoy an updated version of his recipe for a honey omelet a lot better.

Honey Omelet

You'll need: bowl, wisk or fork, 4 eggs, 2 tablespoons (30 ml) olive oil, 10" to 12" (25 to 30 cm) nonstick *skillet* (pan), 3 tablespoons honey (45 ml), pepper to taste

In the bowl, wisk (or beat with a fork) the eggs and blend them with the olive oil until they are well mixed. Heat a little oil in the skillet until it is hot. Add the egg mixture and cook on low until the eggs begin to set. Lift the edges of the omelet with a spatula and let the uncooked egg run underneath. Do not flip the omelet. When the eggs are cooked, flip the omelet onto a plate bottom side up. Drizzle with honey and sprinkle with pepper.

As the Romans said before a good meal — and people still say today — *Buon Appetito!*

Note: Please do this activity with adult supervision.

Fabulous Feasts — and You Are Invited!

At sunset, after the baths, the dinner parties for the wealthy began. First, a slave washed your feet and escorted you into a room decorated with flowers. You'd hop up onto a big flat couch covered with a clean cloth, lean back on one arm, and relax.

This was actually the Greek style of fine dining, copied by the Romans. To Romans, who admired Greek ways, sitting up to eat was *hopelessly* old-fashioned!

On the Menu

Gustatio: First course of **olives, stuffed jellyfish,** and **peacock eggs**

Cena: Second course of **roasted pork, parrot, gazelle,** and **flamingo**

Secunda Mensa: For dessert, **fruit, roses in pastry, dates stuffed with nuts**

Roman Theater

The Romans learned about theater from the Greeks, but they didn't favor serious plays, called *tragedies*. They preferred silly *satires* that made fun of the authorities. Roman writers had to be careful not to make their plays *too* funny, however. That could get them into big trouble!

The only original Roman theater invention is *pantomime*, where a story is acted out with gestures, but no words. Some pantomime was serious and tragic. Is it fun to pantomime? Find out!

Become a Mime

First, choose a story. (Perhaps the legend of Romulus and Remus, Hannibal's story, or Julius Caesar's life story?) Find music to match the mood and drama of your story. Classical music or any wordless music is fine.

To create the pantomime, boldly act out the story with great exaggeration without talking! Use your whole body, your face, *props* (objects), and costumes. Hats instantly turn you into different characters. Gloves highlight hand gestures. Lipstick and eyeliner help exaggerate your facial expressions, which bring out the emotions of the story.

To practice miming, bend your knees and pretend to lift a heavy box off the floor. Let your face show struggle. Grit your teeth and pant, as if the box were almost too heavy to lift. The trick is to fool your audience through the sheer power of your acting.

Ham it up! And don't forget to take a big bow at the end!

Make a Living-Room *Odeum*

If you write a few poems or songs and get your friends to do the same, you can transform an ordinary living room into an extraordinary Roman *odeum*, a place where poetry was read! Set out plenty of flowers in vases and spritz perfume into the air before the guests arrive. (The Romans were very big on perfume — they even put it in their fountains!)

Read from a poem you enjoy and poems of your own.

Try It! The secret of poetry and song lyrics is that they're easy to write! The only rule is that *freedom rules.* Poems do not have to rhyme and they can be sad, silly, or serious — it's up to you!

To get started, take a deep breath (that brings oxygen to your brain) and close your eyes. Let a thought, idea, or picture bubble up in your mind and write about *that*. Sports, vacations, the beach, a walk in the woods, love, hate, loneliness, happiness, fear, sadness, anger, feelings about someone or something, pets, the wind — all of these can be the subject of a poem. You can even write a poem about poetry!

Or, make up some music to go with your poem, and presto! You have a song! There's no limit to creativity at the odeum!

I am Barney. Bark!
Always keep my food bowl full
Where you park the car.

DOGGIE HAIKU*

*A HAIKU (HI-koo) is a Japanese poem consisting of three unrhyming lines of five, seven, and five syllables.

Roman Poets

Pleased to Meet You

The great Roman poets were Virgil, Horace, Ovid, Catullus, and Martial, who lived between the last century B.C. and the first century A.D.

Virgil (Publius Vergilius Maro) went to school with Emperor Augustus, who later asked him to write the story of Aeneas in verse, which later became the famous Aeneid. The eloquent Virgil asked for these words to be on his gravestone: "I sang of pastures, farms, and rulers."

This poem was written during imperial times about a lady named Galla who liked to look good.

The golden hair that Galla wears
Is hers: who would have thought it?
She swears it's hers, and true she swears,
For I know where she bought it.
—MARTIAL, "GALLA'S HAIR"

This poem is about a pet parrot and his best friend, a turtle. What is the stone Ovid refers to?

Our parrot, sent from India's farthest shore,
Our parrot, prince of mimics, is no more.
Mourn all that cleave the liquid skies, but chief,
Beloved turtle, lead the general grief,
Through long harmonious days the parrot's friend,
In mutual faith still loyal to the end!
"His Mistress's Darling" — that his stone may show —
The prince of feathered speakers lies below.
—OVID, "CORINNA'S PARROT"

Come Celebrate!
Roman Holidays and Festivals

On feast days we want to eat, drink and be merry.

— SIGN ON A SHOP IN ANCIENT ROME

How would you like to have 240 holidays in one year? For a period of time in Rome, that's how many there were! That's because the Romans adopted lots of religions as the empire grew. Isis, an Egyptian goddess of life, and Mithras, the Persian god of light and wisdom, were especially popular with the women of imperial Rome. Holidays meant a day off from work, for worship or play.

It's Beginning to Look a Lot Like ... Saturnalia?

A favorite holiday was *Saturnalia*, in honor of Saturn, the god of agriculture. It was celebrated in late December, on the shortest day of the year. The Romans gave the sun god a party so that he would make the days longer again. Saturnalia was a time for merrymaking, gifts, candles, prayer, and homes decorated with holly wreaths.

Hey! Is this beginning to sound familiar?

The early Christians tried to make "Christ's Mass" as much fun as Saturnalia. In the year A.D. 336 they even changed the date of Christ's birthday to December 25 (Mithras's birthday) to attract converts!

Make a Saturnalia Candle

A candle decorated with pressed flowers or leaves was a typical gift at Saturnalia. If you can't wait for pressed flowers, make an updated version with a spare photo.

You'll need: 2 candles (one of which is pillar-style), metal spoon, spare photo

Warm the back of a spoon over a candle by holding the spoon slightly above the flame. Press the back of the warmed spoon to the pillar-style candle where you want to put the photo, until the wax is softened. Position the photo on the candle and gently press it into position.

Note: Please do this activity with adult supervision.

The Circus Maximus

The *Circus Maximus* was a bullet-shaped arena where daredevils raced chariots and horses. It seated more than a quarter of a million people, making it the largest arena *ever!*

Charioteers and horses were decorated with red, white, blue, or green, and the fans rooted for the various colors. These races were like our football and baseball games in terms of fan loyalty, but the audience attraction was *speed* — like NASCAR racing! The chariots raced around the track so fast that workers had to spray water on their smoking wheels! The favorite seats in the arena, called *shipwrecks*, were on the ends, where the chariots and horses crashed into one another.

Imagine how the Romans would have loved video games!

Gruesome Roman Games

Some of what the Romans called games, people of today would call murder and insanity. In Rome, games took place at the beautiful four-story oval *Colosseum*, which still stands today in Rome, Italy. There were similar theaters all over the empire. These games were extremely important to all of the Romans, as a kind of uniting national pastime.

Like today's television shows, there were different kinds of games. But unlike television and movies, there was *real* violence and death at the end. Sometimes ancient stories were "acted" by people — who would *really die* at the end. Sometimes hungry predators, like lions, would pounce on prey (including *humans*) — and *really devour* them.

RUINS OF THE ANCIENT COLOSSEUM IN ROME, ITALY. PEOPLE SAT ON THE STONE SEATS SET BLEACHER-STYLE AROUND THE OVAL.

The games started with "beast hunts" in which animals were forced to attack each other. During the lunch hour came public executions. (How's that for entertainment?) In the afternoon, *gladiators* (who were slaves, criminals, or prisoners of war) fought — and *died* — for the amusement of the crowd. Thumbs-up or thumbs-down from the emperor decided which gladiator lived and who was to be killed.

Year after year, animals and people were tortured, beaten, eaten, or hacked to bits at these gory games. No wonder the exits of the Colosseum were called the *vomitoriums*.

YEA OR NAY?

Have you ever gotten the "thumbs-up" from family or friends after performing something really well or getting a hit, run, or goal in sports? How'd that make you feel?

Violent Entertainment

People are *still* entertained by violence on TV and in the movies. Fortunately, no one gets hurt — at least, not physically. But some experts believe that watching violence is unhealthy. They argue that when people see a lot of violence acted out it begins to seem "normal." They also point to horrible accidents that have occurred when kids tried to imitate actions they saw on screen.

Others argue that viewing violence is perfectly safe. They say that most people know the difference between pretend and reality. When kids get hurt imitating screen violence, these people blame the adults who were supposed to be supervising them.

Take a stand on this important issue. Consider how violent images entering your mind affect you. If you were a debater, could you argue that there is value to viewing violence?

Now be a modern emperor and rule with a thumbs-up or thumbs-down on violence on TV, in video games, or in movies.

Light a Candle for Victims of Violence

When we learn of violence done to humans or animals today, we become upset. That's a normal, natural reaction. But how can we comfort ourselves?

With an adult's permission, light a candle in honor of all mistreated people and animals of the past and present. As the flame brightens the room, hope that the flame of goodness will one day warm the coldest hearts. Make a promise to yourself to work for victory over violence by being kind and by encouraging others to be kind, too.

Spartacus, a Notable Slave

Pleased to Meet You

Spartacus was a gladiator slave who escaped and began a slave rebellion. With an army of runaway slaves, he fought the Roman army for over two years! Although Spartacus and his fellow slaves were punished harshly (more than 6,000 slaves were hanged along the Appian Way!), their actions had a big impact on Roman society. Some wealthy Romans became nervous about having slaves at home.

In the 1960s, a movie, *Spartacus*, was made about this daring person, who took a stand in the worst situation. It's worth seeing!

The Greeks: "Just Say, 'No!' "

When a games' promoter tried to set up a Roman games in Athens, Greece, one man shouted to the audience, "Athenians, before you admit the gladiators, come with me and destroy the altar to the god of pity!"

With that, one by one, the people stood up and went home. The gory games were never played in Greece.

Όχι!*

(* Greek for "NO")

After Augustus Caesar

At the end of his long rule, Augustus claimed, "I found Rome a city of brick and left it a city of marble." (More accurate would be, "I found Rome a city of concrete covered with brick, and I left it a city of concrete covered with marble!")

Augustus's stepson, *Tiberius*, became the next ruler. He had no living sons, so others from the Caesar family were found to rule after him. Some were good and able leaders; others — like Caligula and Nero — were believed to be insane.

Still, thanks to Augustus's principate, the Roman Empire survived even the worst leaders for hundreds of years.

Nifty Teachers Have Apples and Mangoes: The Five Good Emperors

At the end of the *Pax Romana* a line of five so-called good emperors reigned over imperial Rome. To remember their names, remember this phrase: **N**ifty **T**eachers **H**ave **A**pples and **M**angoes.

1. **N**erva invented a way to transfer power peacefully. His method was to have each emperor personally pick and train his successor. He trained …

2. **T**rajan, who was born in Spain. He extended the empire, gave generously to the poor, and trained …

3. **H**adrian, who traveled all over the empire, giving people Roman citizenship. He also limited the growth of the empire in order to concentrate on good government. He trained …

4. **A**ntoninus Pius, who continued the peace and prosperity, made fair laws, and trained …

THE MARITIME THEATRE, PART OF HADRIAN'S VILLA NEAR TIVOLI, ITALY, BUILT IN A.D. 118—125

5. **M**arcus Aurelius, a deep thinker and able leader, who ruled the empire at its most majestic height. When he died, people did not mourn him because they were sure he had gone straight to heaven where he belonged!

In his famous book, *Mediations*, Marcus Aurelius wrote:

"The Universe itself, is change."

And, judging by what was about to happen in the Roman world, times were about to change!

The Roman Empire makes a fine parade, but no one marches in glory forever. Behind them, challenges are coming, and new ideas are creating new ways of life. Come, let's be there to see it happen!

Rome's Decline & Fall

*"Our history now plunges
from a kingdom of gold
to one of iron and rust."*

—Cassius Dio, Roman historian

Rome's slow decline began when Marcus Aurelius allowed his son *Commodus* to rule after him. *Big mistake.* Commodus was called a "greater curse to the Romans than any disease or crime." After 12 years of misrule, he was assassinated.

Then, to the horror of everyday Romans, the palace guards auctioned off the position of emperor! The great empire was actually for sale!

To save the day, the army stepped in and appointed an emperor, *Severus,* who began a new royal line.

Emperors came and emperors went — good ones, bad ones, and ones in-between. And after each one died or was killed, the same old fights broke out again, about who would rule. These costly internal wars were expensive and exhausting.

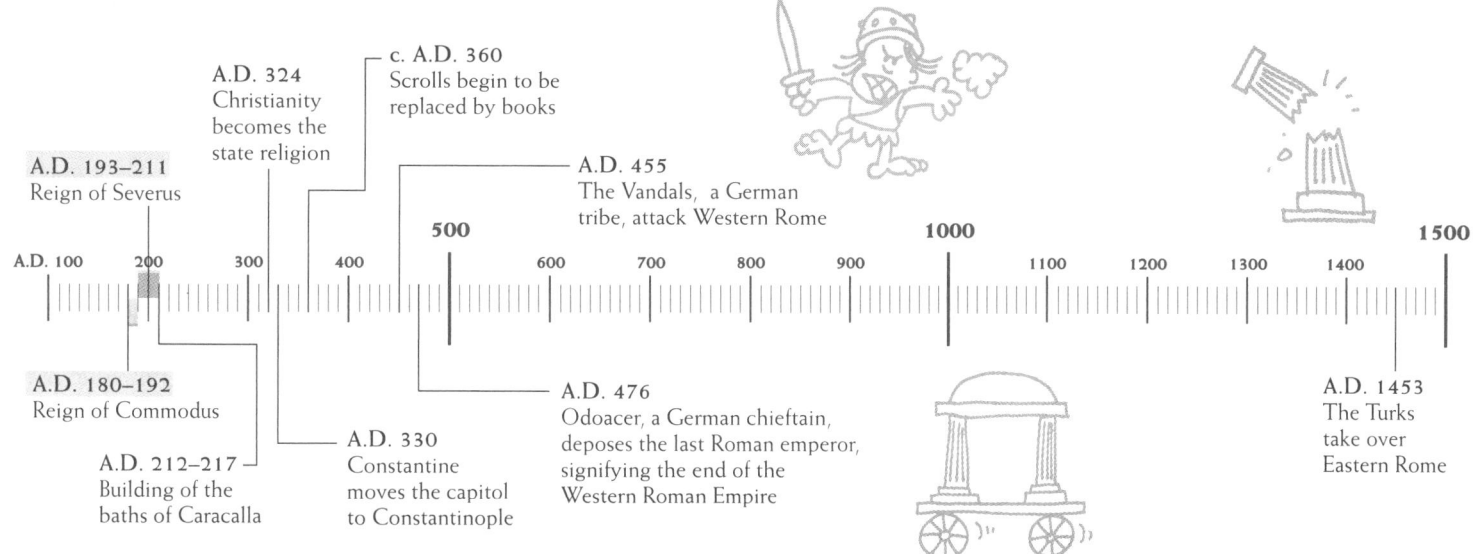

A.D. 324
Christianity
becomes the
state religion

c. A.D. 360
Scrolls begin to be
replaced by books

A.D. 193–211
Reign of Severus

A.D. 455
The Vandals, a German
tribe, attack Western Rome

500   1000   1500

A.D. 100   200   300   400   600   700   800   900   1100   1200   1300   1400

A.D. 180–192
Reign of Commodus

A.D. 212–217
Building of the
baths of Caracalla

A.D. 330
Constantine
moves the capitol
to Constantinople

A.D. 476
Odoacer, a German chieftain,
deposes the last Roman emperor,
signifying the end of the
Western Roman Empire

A.D. 1453
The Turks
take over
Eastern Rome

There were other troubles, too. In Europe, vigorous German tribes, called *Vandals, Goths,* and *Visigoths,* began moving into the empire. Because of famine in some of the Roman provinces, there was a shortage of healthy soldiers to defeat them. Some emperors tried to bribe the German leaders with gold and Roman citizenship. But gold meant little to the Germans, and they didn't want to become Roman, either. The three-step master plan of conquest (page 60) was no longer working.

The Big Picture

After Marcus Aurelius, ordinary Romans probably didn't know that Rome was on the way down. They were busy leading their lives as best they could. The army still patrolled the borders and built roads. The priests still had ceremonies for the gods. People still enjoyed traditions and festivals.

Only by looking back do we see that Roman power and influence were fading. Like the view in a rearview mirror, Rome's *importance* was becoming smaller and smaller; the Roman methods were becoming less and less effective.

Changes: A New Capitol and New Beliefs

One emperor, *Constantine,* built a new capitol across the sea at the old Greek city of Byzantium. The empire had gotten so big that it needed two capitols, one in the east and one in the west. This "Eastern Rome" was complete with Jupiter's temple, baths, a forum, and a coliseum. He called the city *Constantinople.*

Constantine made another giant-sized change in the Roman Empire; he changed the official religion!

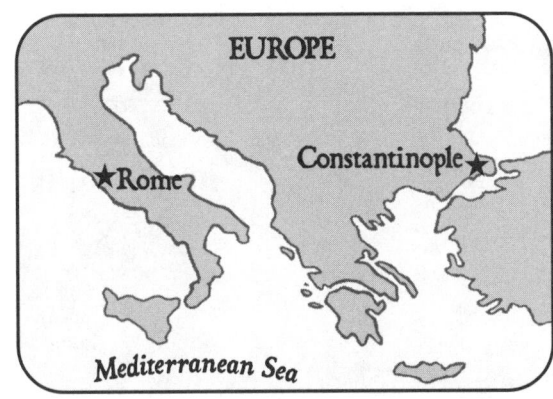

Worldly Words

CITY OF CONSTANTINE

Constantinople is the combination of the Latin *polis* (or *ple*), meaning "city" and the name *Constantine.* It is today's Istanbul, Turkey. In the 1950s there was even a song called "Istanbul" with the lyric "It's Istanbul, not Constantinople now . . ."!

A New Religion

As the Roman world expanded, Roman ideas expanded, too. By the time they had a huge empire, the Romans were no longer simple farmers trying to control the natural forces of life. They were part of a great empire, and they began to wonder about the meaning of life.

The Eastern religions based on the deities of Isis and Mithras fascinated the Romans for a while. But in the end neither those gods, nor the Greek gods, nor even their beloved numina (pages 37–38) could answer the questions they had about life.

In the Roman province of *Palestine*, however, a new religion had been slowly growing. It offered other answers to life's uncertainties: It was called *Christianity*.

PART OF THE PIAZZA SAN PIETRO IN
VATICAN CITY, ITALY, BUILT A.D. 1656–1657

Christianity

Today there are *hundreds of millions* of Christians living all over the world.

But in Roman times, Christianity was just beginning to take root. The Romans, who usually let people worship as they pleased, were upset by the Christians at first. The Romans could not understand why the Christians refused to worship the Roman gods, in addition to their spiritual leader, Jesus. Some emperors blamed the Christians when things went wrong in Rome.

But Constantine, whose mother was Christian, gave land to the church and allowed Christian priests to take over Roman religion. Since Rome had no separation between church and state (in which the leaders of the religions and the leaders of the government are different people), Constantine's actions gave the church incredible power and authority.

A small part of Rome, Italy, today, called *Vatican City*, is home to the Roman Catholic Church. The official name of its leader (the pope) is *Pontifex Maximus*. That is the same name that Romulus gave himself! (It means "Best Bridge Builder.")

Later Roman Laws: A Living Legacy

Just as Roman religion changed over time, so did Roman law. The later laws reflected a deep respect for individual rights. Here is a sample of Roman legal ideas that became part of the Roman legacy (a *legacy* is a valuable gift that is passed down through the generations, like money, a house, or something given by an elder):

▣ No one should suffer for what he thinks.

▣ A father is not a good witness for a son, nor a son for a father.

▣ The punishment should fit the crime.

▣ A person should be considered innocent until proven guilty.

Try It! Can you figure out the basic idea behind each of these laws? Think of legal cases — real or imagined conflicts — that reflect these ideas. Role-play the part of a Roman lawyer who has to use these ideas to defend a client. What would you say to the judge or jury?

The End of the Roman Empire

Eastern Rome lasted as a wealthy power until the Turks took over in A.D. 1453. Until their very last day, the leaders in Constantinople called themselves Roman.

Western Rome fell earlier because it was unable to defend itself from the Germans. In A.D. 455, the *Vandals* ran through Rome, completely wrecking the place — an event that certainly lives on in our language links, as we're sure you noticed!

In A.D. 476 the Vandal king, *Odoacer*, got rid of the last Roman emperor and named himself emperor instead. But he had no wish to be a *Roman* emperor! The days of Roman power were over, but its ruins and its legacies remained.

Oh, no! They're here to vandal-ize us!

The Great Roman Legacy

The Romans may be gone, but their ways live on in the great Roman legacy. Some of the things that survived the destruction of Rome as a legacy for all of humanity include:

▣ **Appreciation of others' creativity and skills**

▣ **Calendars**

▣ **Christianity**

▣ **Conquest without total destruction (except the destruction of Carthage)**

▣ **Engineering feats and architectural firsts (roads and vaulted ceilings)**

▣ **Fine dining and fast food**

▣ **Freedom of religion**

▣ **Justice and laws that try to be fair**

▣ **Latin and Romance languages**

▣ **National and global unity (during the *Pax Romana*)**

▣ **Pantomime**

▣ ***Philanthropy* (giving money for good causes)**

▣ **Preservation of great art (like the ancient Greek art)**

▣ **A representative government**

Plant a Living Legacy

To show the living legacy of positive influences of ancient Rome, make a table centerpiece of ivy cuttings (place each in a slender bottle or a small can filled with water). Each ivy cutting — ivy was a favorite plant of the Romans — will stand for an aspect of ancient Rome that you have selected as valuable and important to you, personally. Your cuttings will take root, just as Roman ideas took root in the world. (When a cutting has many roots, simply plant it in a small pot with potting soil, place on a sunny windowsill, and water it weekly.)

... And the "Not-So-Great"

Of course, not everything that the Romans left was positive, right? Remember the two sides of human nature that lived in every Roman? Aside from the great legacies, they left disturbing, unresolved — maybe unnoticed — troubles like sexism, exploitation of others, a class society that approved of slavery, a need to conquer, power to the wealthy, a love of violence for entertainment, and mistreatment of animals. And we saw a lot of greed and love of power — two very destructive forces in human nature.

So, Is a Look Backward Relevant in Our Forward-Thinking World?

Well, here we are at the end of the Roman Empire. We've seen a city grow on seven hills where two brothers supposedly fought to rule. We saw seven kings rule and a class of wealthy Romans, the patricians, assert themselves, only to be taken to task by the ple-

beians, a group of everyday folk. We saw the Roman Republic function in ways that remind us of republics the world over today.

We enjoyed the *Pax Romana* when Romans lived well for two hundred years, under the rule of emperors. We watched as Rome conquered, but embraced those whom they ruled. And we watched, too, as greed for more and more land and power caused the Romans to lose sight of their plan and their philosophy of preserving what they conquered. And then, a split, a shift in power, and eventually the fall of Rome.

That's a lot to observe in a parade! What stands out in your mind as most memorable? And what is the value in all of this — or is there a value? Did you learn anything that will help you understand yourself and make more sense of your relationships with other people, government, politics, and family and community life?

Does history, and specifically Roman history, speak to you in an important way?

Nothing Lasts Forever … Except Rome?

Six years after the Vandals overtook Rome, a Roman poet wrote that Rome would last

*"So long as earth shall stand,
and heaven uphold the stars."*

Judging from the many Roman influences on our lives today, maybe he was right. All that Rome stood for, its values and its ways — some good and some not-so-good — became the pillars of Western society.

Under those pillars, the great parade of history continues. And *you* are an important part of it!

Index

# More *Kaleidoscope Kids* Books from Williamson Publishing

For ages 7 to 14, 96 pages, fully illustrated, 10 x 10, $10.95 US/ $17.95 CAN.

More books by Avery Hart:

Children's Book Council Notable Book
WHO *REALLY* DISCOVERED AMERICA?
Unraveling the Mystery & Solving the Puzzle
by Avery Hart

Children's Book Council Notable Book
Dr. Toy 10 Best Educational Products
PYRAMIDS!
50 Hands-On Activities to Experience
Ancient Egypt
by Avery Hart and Paul Mantell

Children's Book Council Notable Book
American Bookseller Pick of the Lists
KNIGHTS & CASTLES
50 Hands-On Activities to Experience the
Middle Ages
by Avery Hart and Paul Mantell

American Bookseller Pick of the Lists
Parent's Guide Children's Media Award
ANCIENT GREECE!
40 Hands-On Activities to Experience This
Wondrous Age
by Avery Hart and Paul Mantell

THE LEWIS & CLARK EXPEDITION
Join the Corp of Discovery to Explore Uncharted
Territory
by Carol A. Johmann

Benjamin Franklin Silver Award
GOING WEST!
Journey on a Wagon Train to Settle a Frontier Town
by Carol A. Johmann and Elizabeth J. Rieth

Parents' Choice Recommended
BRIDGES!
Amazing Structures to Design, Build & Test
by Carol A. Johmann and Elizabeth J. Rieth

ForeWord Magazine Book of the Year Finalist
SKYSCRAPERS!
Super Structures to Design & Build
by Carol A. Johmann

American Bookseller Pick of the Lists
¡MEXICO!
40 Activities to Experience Mexico Past and Present
by Susan Milord

Teachers' Choice Award
GEOLOGY ROCKS!
50 Hands-On Activities to Explore the Earth
by Cindy Blobaum

THE BEAST IN YOU!
Activities & Questions to Explore Evolution
by Marc McCutcheon

VISIT OUR WEBSITE!

To see what's new at Williamson and learn
more about specific books, visit our website at:
www.williamsonbooks.com

TO ORDER BOOKS:

You'll find Williamson books wherever high quality children's books are sold,
or order directly from Williamson Publishing. We accept Visa and Mastercard
(please include the number and expiration date).

Toll-free phone orders with credit cards:

1-800-234-8791

Or, send a check with your order to:
Williamson Publishing
P.O. Box 185, Charlotte, Vermont 05445

Please add **$4.00** for postage for one book plus **$1.00** for each additional
book. Satisfaction is guaranteed or full refund without questions or quibbles.
Catalog request: **mail, phone, or e-mail info@williamsonbooks.com**
Prices may be slightly higher in Canada.